Five Minute
Lean

A super-quick guide to improving
your job so much you enjoy it again

David McLachlan

Five Minute Lean

Copyright © 2014 by David McLachlan

All rights reserved. No part of this book may be reproduced or transmitted in any form or by any means without written permission of the author.

ISBN 978-0-9941963-6-1

Contents

A Method, a Law, and a Quote. 1

Five Minute Lean Summary 3

Introduction 5
   1. It All Starts With a Standard Process 7
   2. This Book Itself is a Standard Process. 8
   3. Teach and Share to Build an Incredible Culture 10

1 Define Value 13
Where Lisa Makes a Change 14
   1.1 Value is Determined by the Customer 21
   1.2 Gather Direct Feedback and Indirect Feedback . . . 22
   1.3 Collect and Measure Feedback
       With the Net Promoter Score 26
   1.4 Make Feedback Meaningful
       with Kano Analysis 27
   1.5 Use Feedback to Fix and Guarantee 29

2 Map Your Current Process. 33
Where Lisa Discovers a New Way 34
   2.1 Go to the Gemba 42
   2.2 Use Kaizen and Kaizen Events to
       Help Stakeholder Buy-In. 44
   2.3 Get Your Map Started with a SIPOC. 46
   2.4 Map the Value Stream to Reveal Opportunities . . 50
   2.5 Add Important Data to Your Map 56

3 Reduce Wasteful Steps and Improve Flow 63
Where Lisa Performs a Balancing Act 64
   3.1 Eliminate the Eight Wastes to Improve Flow 75
   3.2 Use Pareto to Find Where to Start 79
   3.3 Solve the Real Cause of the Problem 82
   3.4 Help Your Process Flow with Line Balancing 87

    3.5   Work Towards One-Piece-Flow
(and Reducing Silos or Batching) 92

4 Use a Pull System and Build in Quality 97
Where Lisa Pulls the Trigger...................... 98
- 4.1 Create a Pull System with FIFO, Kanban Triggers and Visual Management 109
- 4.2 Build in Quality with Error-Proofing and Autonomation 115
- 4.3 Level the Workload when Demand Fluctuates... 118
- 4.4 Organise Your Process with Five S 121
- 4.5 Put it Together With Design for Ease of Use 124

5 Implement With a Standard Process and Improve Again......................... 127
Where Lisa Sets a New Standard 128
- 5.1 Create a Future State Value Stream Map 135
- 5.2 Present and Manage Your Change Using an A3 and LCA........................136
- 5.3 Implement With Agile for Fast Iterations and Feedback 140
- 5.4 Create a New Standard Procedure and Checklist for Quality Control..................146
- 5.5 The Power of Incentives — What is Measured and Rewarded Improves 148

Epilogue 157

Appendix 159
Five Minute Lean Summary 159
The Five Minute Catch-up........................160
The House of Lean...............................162
A3 Template 163
Seven Step A3 Problem Solving Process..............164
Further Reading.................................166
Glossary of Lean Terms...........................167

A Method, a Law, and a Quote

LEAN

A business philosophy and method for business process improvement

Occam's Law: Everything should be as simple as possible, but not simpler.

"In God we trust, all others must bring data."
—William Deming

SIX SIGMA

An improvement method meaning just 3.4 defects in every million opportunities

Pareto's Law: 80% of your results often come from 20% of your effort.

"Feedback is the breakfast of champions."
—Ken Blanchard

AGILE

A method of small, fast releases for quick feedback

Parkinson's Law: Work expands so as to fill the time available for its completion.

"What determines behaviour are the incentives for the decision maker."—Charlie Munger

Five Minute Lean Summary

Step 1: Define Value *Lean Enterprise Institute calls this: Specifying Value* 1 Value is determined by the customer 2 Gather direct feedback and indirect feedback 3 Use the Net Promoter Score 4 Use Kano Analysis for Delighters and Dissatisfiers 5 Find out what annoys your customer, fix it and guarantee it	
Step 2: Map Your Current Process *Lean Enterprise Institute calls this: Map* 1 Go to the Gemba 2 Use Kaizen and Kaizen Meetings 3 Get started with a SIPOC 4 Create a Map of your Value Stream to Reveal Opportunities and Waste 5 Add Rework, VA/NVA Steps and Timings (Cycle time, Lead time, Takt time)	
Step 3: Reduce Wasteful Steps and Increase Flow *Lean Enterprise Institute calls this: Flow* 1 Eliminate any of the Eight Wastes 2 Use Pareto Analysis 3 Use Fishbone Analysis and the 5 Whys 4 Perform Line Balancing 5 Work towards One Piece Flow	

Step 4: Use a Pull System and Build in Quality *Lean Enterprise Institute calls this: Pull* 1 Add Visual Management, FIFO and Kanban Triggers 2 Add Poka Yoke and Autonomation for Error Proofing 3 Level the Workload when Demand Fluctuates 4 Use 5S 5 Ensure Design for Ease of Use	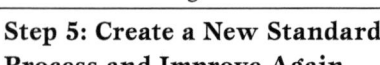
Step 5: Create a New Standard Process and Improve Again *Lean Enterprise Institute calls this: Perfection* 1 Create a Future State VSM and present to decision makers 2 Use an A3, LCA board and an Action Register 3 Use Agile for fast iterations and feedback 4 Create a Standard Operating Procedure and Checklist 5 Change incentives to reflect what you want	

For specific business problems, see the Seven Step A3 Problem Solving Process: page 164

Introduction

This book was created for you.

In fact, if you are working either as an employee or as a business owner there's a good chance you have run into your fair share of frustration over the past year. A recent study found that nearly 87% of employees are "disengaged" in their jobs*, feeling unhappy and stuck with the work they do every day, and I know at times we would probably even use a stronger word for it than that. With the average age of retirement currently in the high sixties and rising, that could be a very long time to spend doing something that you don't enjoy.

This feeling is not just for the majority of employees in the work force either. Small business owners often find themselves working 12-hour days in their business, with no clear process and no way to make things easier for the future. Does any of this sound familiar to you? Perhaps you know someone who is going through the same thing or even someone who feels the same way. Have you ever

---

* From *State of the Global Workplace* by Gallup

come home exhausted because your job makes things more difficult than they should be? Maybe you've been trying to do good work but seem to be blocked at every turn and you think to yourself, "If only there was a better way."

Well here is the good news: There is a better way, and you're about to learn it.

What you are about to learn will help make your job easier, faster, and more enjoyable. It will give you an incredibly simple view of your job or your business and improve it so much that work becomes a pleasure again (or maybe even a pleasure for the first time). It will help you to think like a leader, and people who think and act like leaders tend to get paid more on average than those who don't.

Award winning research[**] has proven that the best of these leaders, in the most outstanding companies around the world, all have the following four capabilities in common:

1. They know how to reveal problems & opportunities in their work
2. They solve the root cause of these problems, building new knowledge
3. They share any knowledge learned throughout the organisation
4. They develop the first three capabilities in others

This book will give you the means to achieve all four of these leadership qualities.

[**] From *The High Velocity Edge* by Steven Spear

INTRODUCTION

It All Starts With a Standard Process

As you will soon discover for yourself, Lean transformations can see incredible results. Process and delivery times can be cut in half (or more), and it is not uncommon for quality to improve in the area of over 100%. But it all starts with a standard process.

Although it might be hard to believe at first, everything in life has a process, whether that process has been properly articulated or not. <u>And where there is a process, it can be improved.</u>

Because of this, I am 100% certain this book can help you, no matter what industry or area you work in.

Top athletes train a very specific way each day to gain the success they enjoy in their field—they have a standard, repeatable process to get results. Restaurants such as McDonalds have built themselves into multi-billion dollar businesses, and are run primarily by 16 year olds at the front line. They can produce food the same way every time, because they have a method that is trained the same way each time to young people on the job.

But it also goes deeper than that.

Surgeons following a process checklist in a study from the New England Journal of Medicine saw death rates drop by almost half (47%). Serious complications also dropped by around 36%. A huge and positive impact, all by following a standard process.

How about music? Surely that is a creative industry, and can't be put in a "standard process" box?

Well, when Lou Perlman started Trans Continental Records in the 1990s, he studied a previously successful band called New Kids on the Block, and discovered that the use of five part harmonies in a certain way resulted in a large number of Top 10 hits. He then used that very same process on the Backstreet Boys, *NSync, Take 5 and O-Town, creating a variety of boy bands from scratch and selling well over 200 million albums between them. It was standard and repeatable and it made him many millions of dollars.

There are many ways standard processes help people to succeed. Starting with your current process and using the methods in this book to improve it has been proven to be *extremely* effective.

This Book Itself is a Standard Process

To make your experience as easy as possible, you'll notice that this book itself is a standard process, which you can reference quickly, depending on where you are on your journey.

Each chapter title is actually one of five individual steps that you can use and see at a glance, based on the five step Lean implementation process at the Lean Enterprise Institute. These steps are "Specifying Value, Map, Flow, Pull, and Perfection". The five sections within each of these chapters are also titled as more detailed instructions for you to reference quickly. Laying out the book in this way ensures that you and your team-mates have the power to learn and share Lean improvement methods in *under five minutes*, and it also makes it easier for you to get started and *learn by doing*, instead of spending time trying to find all of this information yourself.

Included at the beginning of each chapter is also an ongoing story — it is the story of someone improving their job so much that they enjoy it again. As you read this story some parts may seem unusual at first, but please know that they have been carefully crafted to embed in your subconscious the Lean tools and practices. Using a book in this way, with a summary and a story means that people with different learning styles can learn quickly and in the way that they most prefer. Those who prefer a summary can read the summaries, those who prefer a story can read the stories, and those who want it all can read both.

Teach and Share to Build an Incredible Culture

Improving your work not only makes things better and less burdensome for yourself, but it benefits the customer with improved quality and delivery speed, and the shareholders with increased profits and lowered costs as well.

You will notice that when management is on-board and well versed in job-improving tools, they can support and drive a change for the better. When front-line team-mates learn these problem solving skills, they can often see quick ways to improve their job as they already know the process well.

Lean is the common language that when everyone has, ties this all together.

To quickly implement this common language, there is a key underlying principle of Lean, which is "respect for people". Respect for people means that we see problems as an opportunity to improve the *process*; we don't consider it as a failing of the people. Seeing it this way and improving a process also has lasting results — a legacy, even if people come and go.

As more people learn the method, they get a unique combination of front-line expertise and Lean problem solving ability that cannot be bought with money, only grown within your business. This helps the people around you become your greatest asset, and makes it almost impossible for competitors to copy your success as you progress.

Finally, the steps in this book will give you and your team huge benefits in your personal lives. Proof has emerged[***] that shows it is not always extrinsic rewards like money that increases motivation and happiness, but more intrinsic rewards or motivators.

[***] From *Drive* by Daniel Pink

These intrinsic motivators are:

Autonomy
Where we are given free rein in solving a problem

Mastery
Where we can work continuously toward mastering a worthy skill

Purpose
Where we are contributing to something greater than ourselves

A Lean initiative, when taught to every level of a company, can give you all three. By putting this book in everyone's hands, you not only have the power to improve your job, but dramatically increase the engagement of your team-mates across the board as well. Then, not only will work become a pleasure again, but greater financial rewards will begin to flow.

1

DEFINE VALUE

Where Lisa Makes a Change

"I'm going to quit my job."

There was silence on the other end of the phone. Lisa was walking at a brisk pace, as she normally did during her lunch hour. It was a great way to enjoy the bay side and escape the office, not to mention giving her a break from the unrelenting phone calls in the call centre that had made her life so difficult over the last few years.

When Lisa joined the Shoe Emporium five years ago it had seemed like a dream. After all, she was working in a job that paid her to talk about one of her favourite topics — shoes, and it was a small business with an owner who was passionate about the things he created. When they came to work every day, she truly felt like they were changing the world.

Now, as the company grew larger, it was less like a family and more like a business. She shared the floor with more than 300 employees, while shareholders and board directors controlled most, if not all of the decisions. More often than not they were decisions that cut costs and reduced the quality of service to the customers that

Lisa had once loved so dearly. It had made service queues horrendously long and these days it took forever to get anything done, let alone delivered.

So now, there really seemed to be no other choice.

"Hello? Steve, did you hear me? I said I'm going to quit."

Lisa was answered by the sound of loud clanging, grinding and shouting — certainly not what she was expecting. It sounded as though Steve was driving, but if that was the sound of his engine it was clear he wasn't going to get very far.

"Lisa, I heard you," Steve shouted. "But I thought you loved that job? Can you meet for coffee? I'm three blocks away."

"No, I — "

"I'll see you there." Lisa looked at the ended conversation on her phone and rolled her eyes. Steve was not going to talk her out of this one. But one coffee couldn't hurt. Could it?

By the time Steve's beautiful, shiny car limped into the parking lot of their local café, Lisa had already ordered them both cappuccinos and was seated at a table overlooking the bay.

Steve leapt out of the car, brushed himself off as though he was ridding himself of the experience he just had, and sat down. He was a fair looking man with a mop of light brown hair, perhaps in his late forties but wearing an outfit of someone in their late twenties, and with an impossible smile permanently plastered on his face.

Steve had owned a car detailing and tinting service for many years, but it was only recently that things seemed to be going extremely well for him. Which was obviously the reason for the new ride.

"Wow, what a car!" he said. "I'll have to remember that it doesn't seem to like driving over 80 miles per hour on a dirt road, though."

Lisa smiled and shook her head.

Before she had time to respond, a shiny new van pulled up next to Steve's car, and out popped a man in overalls. He looked around, spotted Steve, gave a quick wave as though they'd done this all before and then headed under the hood of Steve's clanging monstrosity that had only just made it into the car park.

Ignoring Lisa's slightly perplexed look, Steve put down his coffee and said: "But more importantly, did I hear you correctly? You said you are quitting your job?"

Lisa's face sunk a little. "I just can't do it anymore, Steve. I know I used to love this job, but with all the cost cutting they've done it's nearly impossible to give my customers a good experience. Some people I've known for years have told me they love talking to me on the phone, but they just can't put up with the poor product and terrible delivery times any longer."

Steve nodded as she spoke.

"Believe it or not, I know exactly what you mean," he said. "In fact that's the reason I wanted to meet — I may have a way to help you."

"Steve," said Lisa, with a serious tone, "I hardly think you detailing cars is the same as me selling shoes."

"They might seem different," considered Steve. "But it wasn't too long ago that I hated the work I did as well. I was doing 12-hour days, constantly having to stay back to fix the work my employees did during the day, cleaning cars and tinting their windows. Customer complaints were also through the roof. It was really terrible!

"Thankfully, that's not where my story ended. The owner of the car sales desk we work with approached me one day and asked if I wanted to 'improve my business so much that I enjoyed it again'. Of course, my answer was yes. I was on my twenty-first straight day and was more than a little delirious."

Steve laughed at himself, and it made Lisa feel better too. He did look a lot happier, she thought, and that made her curious.

"The sales owner showed me a way — a way of streamlining things, making them easier, and standardising them so anyone can do it. I cannot begin to tell you what a huge difference it made. Most of my employees started working with the new streamlined standard, and the ones that didn't, left. It even cost me less per car, so I could reduce my prices a little and beat my competition. Now I even get home on time, every day. It's wonderful!"

Lisa beamed at her old friend. "Steve, that's great!" she said. "But how does that apply to me? I don't tint or detail cars. I just sell shoes in an online store call centre. And I don't have employees — I'm not even the boss where I work."

"That's true Lisa, but there is one thing both our companies share, and that's a process for doing things. The sales desk owner told me that everything has a process, and even though the processes are different, the way we fix them is the same.

"Besides, you can't quit your job. What about your bills, your mortgage, and your family? I know you want to leave, but other jobs aren't always easy to find."

Lisa's face sunk as he said the words, and reality slowly crept in. She was behind on most bills as it was. As much as she thought she wanted it, being unemployed wasn't really an option.

Steve gave her a sympathetic smile. "If this works, it could really change your life for the better. What do you think? Do you want to give it a try?"

Lisa nodded. "Well if I can't quit my job, Steve, I might as well improve it."

"Great!" And the look on Steve's face seemed to make the day brighter already. He paused for a moment in thought.

"You know, there are a few things we can do to get started straight away," he said.

"How did I know you were going to say that?" Lisa said, and she smiled slightly and shook her head.

"I wouldn't usually start so soon, but if we're going to improve your job, we really need to know what your product is."

"Well that's easy," said Lisa. "You already know I sell shoes. Wouldn't that be my product?"

"Not always," said Steve. "You see, your product is what brings value to your customer. And to find out what truly brings them value, you have to ask. Most people think they know, but when they ask their customer they often find a different answer altogether.

"Let me show you what I mean," Steve continued, and he looked over his shoulder and shouted to the van mechanic under his car that he seemed to know so well.

"Hey Nathan!"

"Yeah?" the mechanic yelled back from under the hood of the car.

"What sort of flowers should I get for my daughter's wedding?"

Nathan stopped what he was doing and looked out from under the hood. "How should I know?" he said, a little bewildered, and got back to work.

"Exactly," said Steve pointedly as he turned back to Lisa with a smile.

"You wouldn't ask a mechanic what to do for your wedding. And to find out what value means to your customer, you need to ask your customer."

Lisa nodded her head as she took all this in. "Ok, Steve. I get your point. You know, I talk to enough customers during the day so I'm sure it won't be too hard to ask them one more question, and find out what value means to them."

Steve smiled. "And once we know that, we can really get started."

Lisa looked down at her watch, and wrinkled her nose. "Time to get back," she said.

"But you'll give it a shot?" asked Steve.

"I'll give it a shot," Lisa nodded.

"Great!" said Steve, and he downed the last of his coffee in one gulp.

1.1

Value is Determined by the Customer

"Value is determined by the customer, and to find out what they value we need to ask."

The first step on our journey is a simple one — we need to define what value means to the customer, to ensure our product or process provides that value.

If you want to start revealing process improvement opportunities straight away, you can jump to Chapters Two and Three, however the reason we start here is that when it comes down to it, customers are the reason we are in business. Happy customers mean a happier workplace, and ultimately they pay the bills by buying our product or service. By properly defining value, we can give them an experience they will love, and everybody wins.

"Customer" in this case doesn't just have to be the end customer who buys a product or service. It can also be any person or department downstream, or next in the process from you, as they receive the benefit of your work. In Lean terms, "suppliers" are upstream (before) people or departments, and "customers" are downstream (after).

At the Lean Enterprise Institute, this first step is referred to similarly as "Specifying Value". Whatever you decide to call it, there are three main things you need to know:

- The product is something that brings value to the customer,
- Value is defined as something the customer is willing to pay for, and;
- To find out what value is, we need to ask, or get feedback.

We will go through all of these in this chapter.

If you are an employee like Lisa, this first step should be fairly easy. The process you go through for your customers on a daily basis to create your product or service is most often what brings them value. Adjusting a product, or adding additional value, can be done using the tools in this chapter, and it starts with gathering feedback (1.2).

1.2

Gather Direct Feedback and Indirect Feedback

"By gathering feedback from our customer we can provide the value that they are willing to pay for."

If the product is something that brings value to the customer, how do we find out what value actually means to them?

We need to gather feedback, both directly from the customer by asking, and indirectly in the form of measuring results.

Indirect Feedback — Measuring Customer Results

In Lean, there are certain results, called the "Customer Driven Metrics", which can show us whether a process is working well or not, and also help us clearly define any problem before we begin (3.3). Almost every improvement opportunity within a business can be defined using these metrics, as they are centred on our most important participant, the customer.

They are:

Quality

An increase in the quality of the product or service (or reduction in defects or rework)

Delivery

Making the delivery faster, or better suited to the customer, including faster "delivery" between each process (or improving timings such as Cycle time and Lead time in 2.5).

Cost

A decrease in the cost of creating the product or service, which is ultimately related to Quality and Delivery as well.

Of course, Quality, Delivery and Cost are not the only things that can be can measured. Another great way to see whether a product is providing the right value to the customer is to gather feedback on the metrics below:

Sales
When there is a product, even a Minimum Viable Product for a start-up company, we can measure the sales of the product as we change or add features to it. In this case, the more sales the better.

Returns
While not traditionally considered a good thing, if a product is being returned this is still feedback that we can use, and can also be a good opportunity for us to ask our customer more about what brings them value.

Customer Complaints
Complaints are the perfect way to measure if a product is performing well. Obviously, the fewer the better. They are also a goldmine for Lean initiatives because where there is a complaint, there is an opportunity to improve, so we should collect complaints and use them wisely.

Direct Feedback — Asking Our Customer

Alternatively, the most straight forward way to get feedback from a customer is to ask. And typically the best time to ask a customer for feedback is after they have bought the product or service and the experience is fresh in their minds — for example when Lisa has been through a sales call with one of her customers.

Depending on the situation, we can use:

1. Asking face to face
2. Telephone follow-up calls
3. Email follow-ups
4. Customer surveys
5. An online question box
6. A feedback slip to collect or place in a box

Sections 1.3, 1.4 and 1.5 go into more detail as to what to specifically ask your customers, and how to manage the results you get.

1.3

Collect and Measure Feedback With the Net Promoter Score

"The Net Promoter Score is a great way to discover and measure customer value."

The Net Promoter Score (NPS) was outlined in a book called "The Ultimate Question 2.0" and is a great way to determine customer feedback and what they truly value.

It is a simple question we can ask when we want to gather direct feedback, typically after the product or service has been delivered.

- On a scale of one to 10 how likely would you be to recommend us to a friend?

Let's say a customer says a "six". The next question works both because of its simplicity and its results:

- What would it take to make it a 10?

When a customer answers this question for us, it prompts them to give more detail on what would bring them enough value to compel them to recommend our services. This question can be used in a survey, or as a follow up call to the customer to ensure we try and fix the problem straight away.

Using the NPS in this way is a great start in finding out what delights and what dissatisfies our customer, which brings us to Kano Analysis in our next section:

1.4

Make Feedback Meaningful with Kano Analysis

"By discovering what delights our customers we can do more of it, by discovering what dissatisfies our customer we can fix it."

Alternatively to the Net Promoter Score, we can ask the following two questions to discover what delights or dissatisfies our customer:

- What did you love about your experience?
- What did you hate about your experience?

This gives us enough information to be able to separate the answers into three sections:

- Delighters (things customers love, or anything mentioned with an NPS score of eight or above),
- Satisfiers (NPS scores between five and eight), and;

- Dissatisfiers (things customers hate, or NPS scores of four or below).

Where traditional Kano analysis focuses on basic needs, expected needs and exciting needs of the customer, quantifying our customer feedback using an actual number (NPS) and broadening the scope to include things the customer dislikes gives us much more room for improvement. The aim over time then becomes to increase the things that delight the customers, continue doing the things that satisfy them and reduce the things that dissatisfy them.

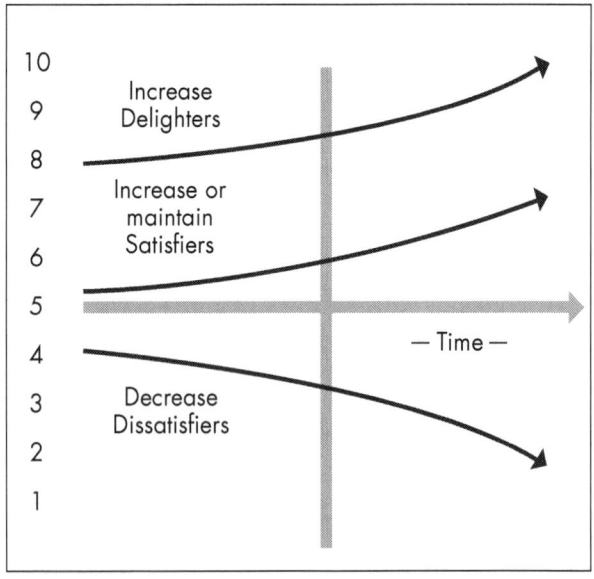

Figure 1: Slightly different to traditional Kano analysis, separating the "Voice of the Customer" into Delighters, Satisfiers, and Dissatisfiers using the Net Promoter Score results can give us more information to improve. The aim becomes, over time, to increase Delighters, maintain or increase Satisfiers, and reduce Dissatisfiers.

You will probably notice that the answers we get in general will also fall into our three Lean "Customer Driven Metrics", which are things that improve on Quality, Cost or Delivery times.

The next section focuses on the one most people would rather avoid — customer "Dissatisfiers" — and how we can actually use these to our advantage.

1.5

Use Feedback to Fix and Guarantee

"Fixing and guaranteeing the things our customer finds annoying is an immensely powerful way to gain raving fans."

Many industries will have their pet hates — things that have become almost clichés as they annoy customers in that industry the most. Perhaps you've had the cable technician who never turns up on time, or the call centre operator who moves slower than a glacier. Great companies and businesses that survive the longest are ones that take this into consideration and do something about it.

One of the most simple and powerful methods we can use here is to:

Find out what annoys the customer most

Discover what annoys your customer by using the Net Promoter Score "Dissatisfiers", and collecting customer complaints. Examples of this step might include a tradesperson that doesn't show up, clothes bought from an online store that don't fit, or food that is cold when it's delivered.

Fix it

Imagine if your tradesperson actually did show up right on time, every time? Or your clothes were either the right size or you could exchange them? Or your food really was delivered hot and fresh for every order? We can fix what annoys your customers the most using the tools in this book.

Then guarantee it

Now imagine if your tradesperson showed up on time, *guaranteed*? Or your clothes were the right size or you could exchange them for free, *guaranteed*? Or your food was delivered hot and fresh *guaranteed,* or it's free?

These three steps are truly one of the fastest ways to get yourself raving fans, and raving fans turn average earnings into outstanding earnings.

The examples above were not just chosen at random either — they are real life examples of outstanding companies. Domino's Pizza implemented the idea of pizza delivered in 30 minutes or it's free, *guaranteed* and the company has gone from strength to strength in business and in its stock price since.

Zappos is an online clothing and footwear company that implemented a 365 day return policy (effectively a satisfaction *guarantee*), and has grown from a small online store to turning over more than a billion dollars a year.

And lastly, local tradespeople who show up on time, *guaranteed*, have more work than they need and can often charge more than the average as well.

When you combine all of the five steps in "Define Value" you have a quick and easy way to get insight into what brings your customer value and what they would be willing to pay for. This is truly powerful information, and can save you a lot of heartache down the track, whether you are just starting a business or improving an existing one.

2

MAP YOUR CURRENT PROCESS

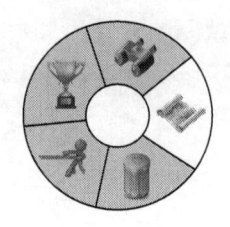

Where Lisa Discovers a New Way

Lisa sat at her keyboard, enjoying a bagel before her shift started at 7AM. As she flicked through her dozens of emails, meeting requests and other things that never got looked at or finished, she saw one that caught her eye:

>To: All Service Centre Employees

>Subject: Urgent Notice Regarding Your Employment

"As you all know, at the Shoe Emporium we have strived to be the first choice for passionate shoe buyers over the past five years.

Unfortunately, to remain cost competitive in a tough market, the board of directors have made the difficult decision to cease the employment of all northern service centre employees by the 14th of next month.

If you are receiving this email, then this decision relates to you."

Lisa stopped reading and put down her bagel. "Cease the employment?" She was being downsized! Lisa had known things were bad at the Shoe Emporium, but being put out of a job like this was the last thing she had expected, and the 14th was less than four weeks away.

Lisa checked her watch, picked up her phone and dialled a number. If she timed it just right she would have 20 minutes before the call centre opened. The phone only rang once.

"Hi you're on the phone with Steve," said the perpetually cheerful voice on the other end.

"Hi Steve," Lisa said, trying to keep her voice steady. "They just announced something big here. Can I meet you at the boardwalk?"

"You can, because I'm actually here right now," said Steve, but he didn't get to finish before Lisa hung up her phone and quickly headed down to meet him.

At the boardwalk near the bay, the people were blissfully unaware of Lisa's news. As she made her way through the holiday makers strolling leisurely about, she saw Steve standing by a large sign, there as promised.

"These things are just fantastic," said Steve as Lisa approached, and she looked up to see that the large sign he was looking at was in fact a map of the bay area.

"Steve, they've just announced they're cutting costs," said Lisa, slightly out of breath. "All the bay area call centre employees are going to be losing their jobs in four weeks, including me."

"Cost cutting eh?" Steve furrowed his brow for a moment in thought. "Never a good sign. And even worse, I suppose, when you're not on the end doing the cutting," he added sympathetically.

"Steve, what am I going to do?"

Steve was silent for a moment, lowered his chin and looked across at her solemnly.

"Well, Lisa, you know we were both going to be doing this process improvement anyway," he said. "If we were going to do it before, would you be willing to still do it now to save your job?"

Lisa paused to let the words digest. This certainly wasn't the option that first came to mind. Save her job in four weeks? Surely it could not be possible. But... what was the alternative?

"Well," said Lisa. "I guess I have no choice but to say yes."

"You always have a choice, Lisa," said Steve. "I know it might sound crazy, but I've seen this thing work wonders. There is a lot I have to teach you, but I think together we could do it."

"Well I've got about five minutes now," said Lisa, a smile finding its way to her face. "Will that suit?"

Steve laughed a deep, warm laugh. "Five minutes eh?" he said, obviously up to the challenge. And then seeming to remember something, he said: "Well we can start here, with this map."

He looked again at the large map of the bay area. Printed down the bottom were the words: "YOU ARE HERE" next to an arrow in bold.

"This was the next thing I was going to teach you, Lisa," said Steve. "I came here for a reason, you see. Because if we want to get anywhere worth going, we first need to know where we are."

Lisa looked at him sceptically. "Doesn't that sound like something a monk might say, not a business owner? No offense Steve, but I'm about to lose my job here and I'm almost late for work."

Steve laughed. "I promise, you will love this. Let's head back to your building while we talk.

"You see most businesses don't know or haven't articulated their current processes — they just let their employees work and hope for the best. They can't improve their business because they don't even know where they currently are.

"You might say they are lost without a map."

Lisa's brow unfurrowed a little as she warmed to the idea. "A map," she said, half to herself. "But what kind of map?"

"A process map, Lisa. A map of the things you do that bring value to your customers."

"Oh, of course. And we all know value is determined by the customer," said Lisa, in a mock sing-song voice.

"Aha! The perfect student—you remembered!" Steve smiled his unstoppable smile.

"You know how I remember that?" asked Lisa. "I actually took your advice and asked my customers what they like and want more of. And you know, I found out a few things I wouldn't have if I'd just assumed."

"Oh?" Steve raised an eyebrow, even more interested.

"I found out a lot of my customers would be willing to pay for faster shipping," Lisa continued. "So that would add value. They would also pay for a longer return period. The majority of my customers tended to shop with us because we had access to really special, niche brands that others didn't. But the main process, of course, was selling shoes."

"That's great! Wow, you've done a great job so far. And for all of those valuable processes, we can create a map."

They sped up slightly as they passed a small boat at the dock. A young crew dressed in white polo shirts were passing boxes of inventory along a gang plank to each other onto the boat. It was a simple process, left to right, left to right until it got to the end.

"Take that boat crew for example," Steve pointed to the crew.

"When we are creating our map, just like that boat we need all our team-mates to be on board or our boat won't run. In other words, we need to include our team-mates from the front lines. And see how they're passing those boxes along to each other? That is exactly how we draw in our processes — moving along from station to station, from process step to process step until it is delivered at the end to the customer."

"I think I get it," said Lisa, and she looked at her watch. Time was running out before the call centre opened and she needed to start work.

"Maybe it would be easier if you could see one," said Steve. "If you've got a few minutes and a spare whiteboard, I'll show you how to make a map now if you like?"

Lisa hesitated just a little. "OK, Steve, but we need to hurry." And they entered the building.

❋ ❋ ❋

Fifteen minutes later, the two were totally engrossed in the rough process map on the whiteboard they had drawn in a spare meeting room at the Shoe Emporium. It seemed simple enough. There was a box with a pointy roof on the left, an arrow moving down and then a row of boxed process steps from left to right.

A few arrows here or there indicated "redoing" a few of the steps, and underneath it all were some rough timings of the steps and queues in between.

"It's amazing," said Lisa, slightly slouched in her chair. "I can see the process. You know, Steve, this might actually help."

"I guarantee it will," said Steve. "But remember, include your team-mates and help get them on board. An important part of Lean is to take them on the journey with you and pass on your knowledge as you make changes. Also, you never know when you will need their support."

Lisa gave him a worried look. "That's the hard part. I don't know anyone who cares enough about their job here to spend time on the process with me. Most of the people are out the door the second their shift is over."

"That may be true, but you must find a way, Lisa."

It was heartening, even if she didn't quite believe it. And for a moment Lisa felt as though it could work. But the moment was broken by the door being flung open — no knock, just a loud crash as it hit the adjacent wall.

"WHO...IS...THIS?" said an overweight, red-faced man pointing directly at Steve. He needed no introduction to Lisa — his name was Robert, and he was Lisa's boss.

Steve turned to the large man without missing a beat and smiled.

"I'm the repair man, your process is broken," he said, arm outstretched for a handshake.

Looking slightly perplexed, Robert pushed aside his open palm and stepped out of the doorway.

"Get out of this office, NOW!" he yelled. And then directing his anger at Lisa, he said: "You are 20 minutes late, the phone lines opened at seven!"

Oh my God, Lisa thought. The time must have slipped away while they were doing their process map.

As they walked out of the office Robert said — voice still well above normal volume — "And you can make up the time tonight. We'll be rounding it UP to an hour with no pay!"

The storm that was Robert the Boss then whisked away to berate someone else.

"I am so sorry about that," said Lisa, as she quickly walked Steve out of the building. "But he's right, I am late. I have to get back."

She managed a half smile. "Thanks for meeting me. There's a lot to take in but I'm sure it will help," she said, not sure at all.

"You can do it, Lisa," Steve said warmly.

With that, they said their goodbyes.

But as Lisa made her way back to her desk, her worry grew. With a boss like Robert constantly around to block any changes she tried to make, what could she do?

She would need some more skills if she was going to succeed.

❂ ❂ ❂

2.1

Go to the Gemba

"To truly know a process we must go to where the work is done — second hand information will not suffice."

Now that we know what brings our customer value from chapter one, we can use the following tools to map out the process of creating that value so everyone can see it clearly and use it to move forward. For this reason, the Lean Enterprise Institute calls this step "Map", and a good map will also reveal opportunities, problems and "waste" (3.1) in a process. We will go through all of these in this chapter.

We also started this book by saying that most businesses don't have an existing standard, repeatable process for their work. Mapping the process is an easy way to articulate the current way of working, to use as a makeshift standard process before you start improving it. After all, you can't improve something you don't have.

First, in order for us to truly know a process we have to go to where the work is done. In Lean this is called going to the "Gemba", and Gemba is the Japanese word for "Actual Place".

In a Lean transformation, getting reports on a situation or hearing it from someone else (like a team-mate or a manager reporting to you) is not good enough. To find out the true situation we must go and experience it first-hand, preferably every day.

This could mean:

- Walking the Gemba (going directly to where the work is done), spending time with the people and asking questions or mapping the process as you go.
- Involving people from the front lines in a Kaizen Event (2.2) as you map a process and get to the root cause of problems, and;
- To a lesser degree, using an LCA Board (5.2) to track metrics of front-line processes.

But it doesn't just mean going to where the work is done. It also means that we "go and see" as soon as a problem occurs, so we can get our team-mates' consensus on what the problem might be before we try and solve it. While this may seem like more work initially, it will save you many hours of wasted effort in the future as a problem gets older or becomes embedded in the workplace culture.

If you are an employee like Lisa, you will already be very familiar with your process, and this book will give you a great way to visualise problems and the tools you need to solve them. If you are a manager or an owner like Steve, you may be more removed from the front-line process during the course of your daily work, which is another reason why learning to regularly go to the Gemba to see and experience for yourself is worth many times its weight in gold.

If you are not sure of a problem, or even a solution, nothing can replace the experience of actually going to where the work is done.

2.2

Use Kaizen and Kaizen Events to Help Stakeholder Buy-In

"Kaizen, and Improvement Events get the right people involved all at once, to properly define the problem and map the path to a solution using Lean tools."

The term "Kaizen" is Japanese for improvement, or continuous improvement.

A Kaizen Event, therefore, means an "improvement meeting". It often involves a few front-line staff from the process involved, a few people who are not familiar with the process to get an outside perspective, and sometimes a few people from the leadership team. Your team use any of the tools they need to from this book, to reveal problems, discover opportunities and make a solid case for change.

If everyone is already familiar with the concepts (and with a book like this in everyone's hands, they should be), then it is much easier to get everything down on paper quickly. It could be started over a cup of coffee with someone involved in the process, or integrated into an existing regular weekly meeting with a team of front-line staff.

Ensuring front-line team-mates and leaders are involved with your Kaizen events will also help you get one of the most important and often the most elusive things: stakeholder buy-in. The more input someone has into something, the more likely they are to support it. As you take them through the steps, you are not only building their skill-set, but helping them be a real part of the solution.

This is why Steve was so insistent on Lisa getting her team-mates involved when starting with her current state map.

By itself, Kaizen or continuous improvement should be a regular part of your week, including "every person, every day" in stopping when there are problems (4.2), defining them using the customer driven metrics (1.2), getting to the real cause of the problem (3.3), and checking ideas to fix them. Even small ideas that warrant a "just do it" test (easily done using Agile, 5.3) to quickly see if they work, can get things underway.

Figure 2: A Lean practitioner leading a Kaizen Event, involving people who do the process every day.

2.3

Get Your Map Started with a SIPOC

"A SIPOC shows you the basic process steps, as well as your customers, requirements and handover points, all at a glance."

One of the fastest ways to get started in mapping a process is with a SIPOC. This kind of map gives us a very simple, high level view to help us begin. If you want a more detailed view, you can use a Value Stream Map (2.4).

SIPOC stands for Suppliers, Inputs, Process, Outputs, and Customer. It allows us to see the basic process flow, the suppliers and customers, and the inputs and outputs for each step. This information can be extremely useful, for example:

- We can quickly see the connections between our process steps
- We can see what is needed to perform our steps correctly
- We can also manage risk efficiently, as we are seeing interacting points that might be affected by any changes we make.

In other words, when our SIPOC is filled out, we can see a large amount of information about our process at a glance.

The first thing we do in our SIPOC is a high level process flow — the main steps we perform to create our product or service. For the sake of continuity, let's use the process flow from the Shoe Emporium in our story:

Supplier	Inputs	Process	Outputs	Customer
		1. Call centre operator takes sales call		
		2. Forms department sends forms to customer		
		3. Processing department takes payment		
		4. Outgoing requests items		
		5. Warehousing sends items		

Figure 3: *The basic process flow outlined in our SIPOC, based on the Shoe Emporium sales process.*

In a SIPOC we are describing only the main steps — as you would if you were telling someone you just met at a barbeque, about your job. Once we have a high level process flow, we can add the Supplier, Input, Output and Customer for each step as well. Remember — our Supplier can be any step before the current one, and our Customer can be any step after our current one.

Supplier	Inputs	Process	Outputs	Customer
End Customer, via telephone	Customer request	1. Call centre operator takes sales call	Request sent to forms department	Forms department
Call centre	Call centre request	2. Forms department sends forms to customer	Forms sent to customer	Processing department
End Customer	Forms sent back by customer	3. Processing department takes payment	Payment taken, request to out-going dept.	Outgoing department
Payments dept.	Item request on customer form	4. Outgoing requests items	Item request in system	Warehousing
Outoing dept.	Item request in system	5. Warehousing sends items	Item shipped	End customer

Figure 4: Our SIPOC with the additional information included so we can see our inputs and outputs at a glance.

We can also add "Customer Requirements" (which are the required outputs of the process), and "Measures", or how the process is measured so we know when it is successful or completed. This additional information is also very useful, and would make our diagram a SIPOCr+M.

Now that we have a high level view of our process, we discover problems in our work with a Value Stream Map.

2.4

Map the Value Stream to Reveal Opportunities

"Mapping the process in this way, we can see the entire process at a glance, including any blockages or sticking points to fix."

A Value Stream Map (VSM) is a map of the flow of steps for creating our product or service. It can be done at a high level, between departments or a low level, in a single task. Because of this, mapping the value stream is a good way to create a standard operating procedure (5.4), if one doesn't already exist. This is also the method that Steve taught to Lisa and encouraged her to try with her teammates, and in doing so they revealed a number of problems and opportunities.

In fact that is the reason we map our value stream: to reveal opportunities in our process for us to improve. Things like long process times, many queues, having to redo work, or information travelling between too many departments. All of this is referred to as "waste", which we go into in more detail in (3.1).

You should know that there is a lot of information packed into the next two sections, and learning how to make a value stream map can seem daunting at first. However, at the end you will be able to see your process at a glance, and it is a very powerful tool.

When creating a VSM, the easiest part to grasp is noting the process steps down the bottom, in order from left to right. Before that, the customer is noted in the top right hand corner, and the supplier is noted in the top left hand corner.

Let's take a look at something simple to start with — our first "SIPOC" step, or Lisa taking a sales call at the Shoe Emporium.

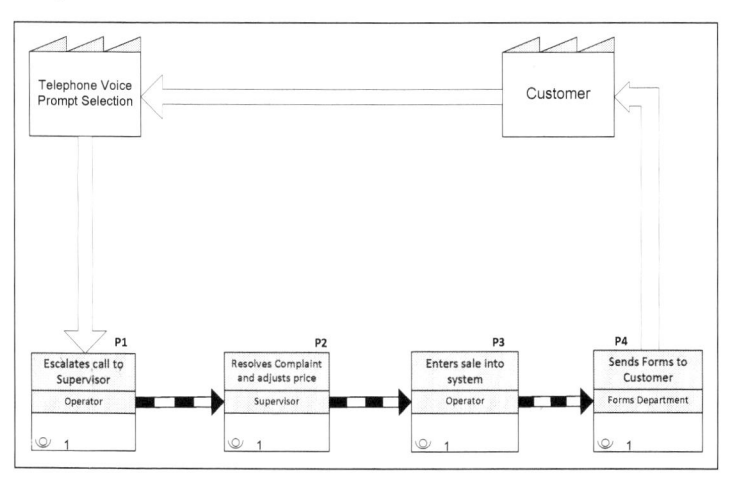

Figure 5: A basic start of a Value Stream Map for the Shoe Emporium sales process. The stream "supplier" is in the top left, the steps are bottom left to right, and we ultimately deliver to the customer again in the top right, completing the cycle.

As you go through the chapters in this book all of this will make more sense to you. Below are a few of the common icons you might come across in a Value Stream Map for you to reference as we progress.

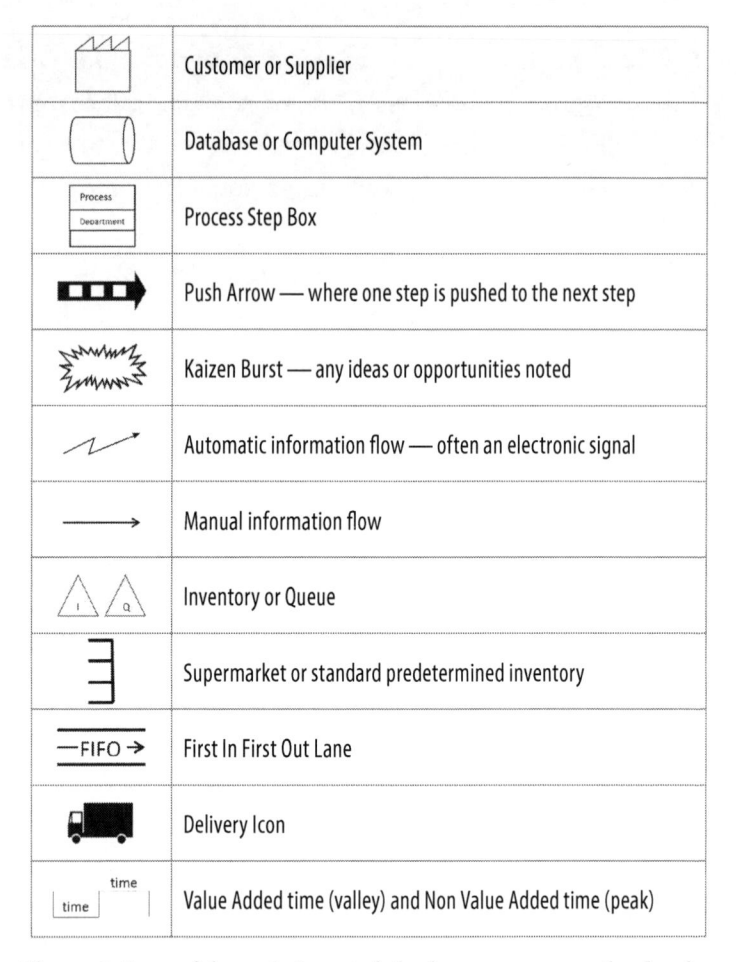

	Customer or Supplier
	Database or Computer System
Process / Department	Process Step Box
	Push Arrow — where one step is pushed to the next step
	Kaizen Burst — any ideas or opportunities noted
	Automatic information flow — often an electronic signal
	Manual information flow
	Inventory or Queue
	Supermarket or standard predetermined inventory
—FIFO→	First In First Out Lane
	Delivery Icon
time / time	Value Added time (valley) and Non Value Added time (peak)

Figure 6: *Some of the main Icons to help show your process clearly when creating a Value Stream Map.*

A picture says a thousand words, so let's add some of these icons in where they belong, and we can see how they work in our Value Stream Map.

MAP YOUR CURRENT PROCESS

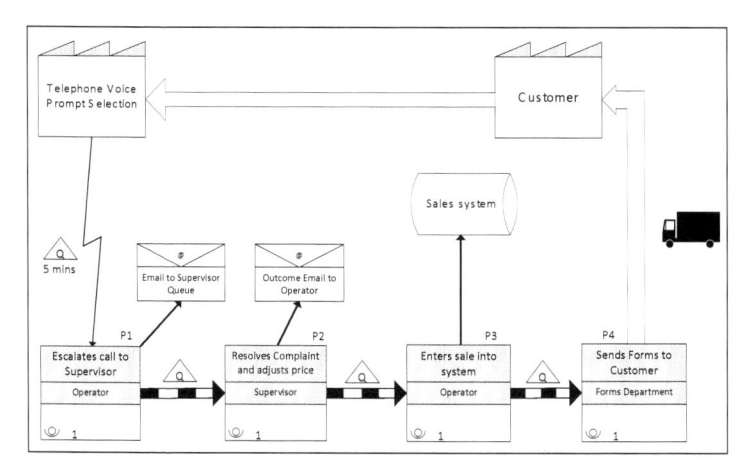

Figure 7: *Our Value Stream Map with added systems, email communication, queues and delivery. With a little experience a map like this will be second nature to you.*

We now can see queues in between our processes, an email communication, an automatic transfer of information from the telephone prompt, databases or systems for where our information is stored, and a truck icon at the end, showing the delivery of the forms to our customer to end this part of the process.

Swim Lane Flow Charts

For those of you who are not yet comfortable with a Value Stream Map, another way of mapping a process is to use a Swim Lane Flow Chart. Also known as a Business Process Map (BPM), it's called a Swim Lane Chart because it looks like an Olympic swimming pool — but don't be deceived by how simple it seems. This method of mapping a process is also extremely powerful.

Different departments or stations are noted on the left from top to bottom with their lanes extending to the right. It's in these lanes that each step is noted, and the steps move up or down the lanes depending on who is performing the step. A picture will help:

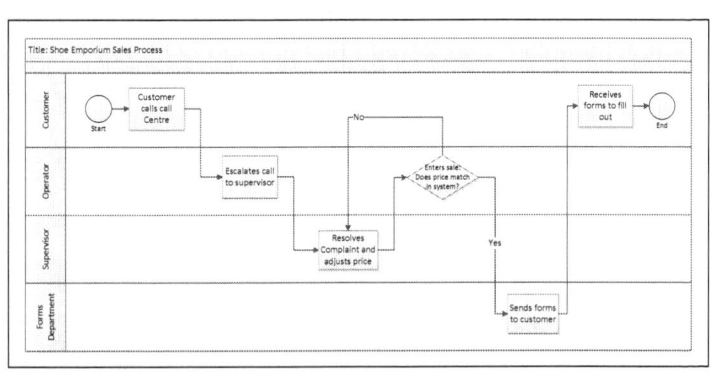

Figure 8: *A basic example of a swim lane flow chart, used to map our value stream. The departments are vertical (up/down) and the process steps are horizontal (left to right).*

The main difference is in the process boxes, where a square is a normal process, a diamond is a decision box (often posed as a "yes or no" question) with one or more pathways and a circle is the start or end of a value stream.

Figure 9: The three main types of process boxes in a Swim Lane Flow Chart. A decision process step is often posed as a "yes or no" question, with the answer influencing where the process goes from there.

You can often get a good idea of the process at a glance using this method. It is also very easy (once you have the hang of it) to quickly jot a Swim Lane Flow Chart down on a napkin or piece of paper over a cup of coffee with front-line team-mates. Next, we add some more information to our map so we can see any opportunities to improve at a glance.

2.5

Add Important Data to Your Map

"Including the right information on your process map allows you to see areas where you can improve straight away."

The last step in "Map" is adding the right information to our Value Stream Map so we can reveal problems and improve the process. This data includes:

- Rework or defects
- Additional problems or ideas called out by front-line staff
- Non-value added steps
- Process and customer timing

Let's look at each one in turn, and then an example at the end.

Rework Percentages

Rework can also be known another way as "First Pass Yield" or "First Time Right". Basically, this is how many times you need to go back through the previous steps to get additional information or fix a defect, for example a car that needs repainting, or a form that is not filled out correctly and needs more information from the previous department.

If our item goes through correctly 70% of the time, then we have a "First Pass Yield" of 70%. Or, if you prefer, you can note it as rework, which is one of the wastes we go into in (3.1) and in which case it would be reworked 30% of the time.

Kaizen Bursts

You will notice in our Value Stream Map icons that there is an icon called Kaizen Burst. A Kaizen Burst icon is a great way to write down additional ideas or problems called out by our front-line team-mates.

We can then delve deeper into these additional problems and solutions when we move into root cause analysis (3.3) and brainstorming solutions.

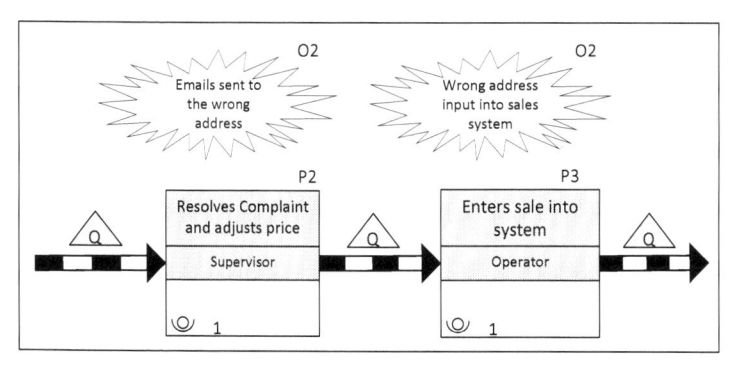

Figure 10: Examples of using Kaizen Bursts to call out opportunities for improvement. Note that we number opportunities to correspond with the process step they relate to.

Value Add / Non Value Add Steps

If the process task improves the product, or the experience of the customer and it is something our customer is willing to pay for, we consider it Value Add (VA). Almost everything else is Non-Value Add (NVA) or waste that we can seek to reduce.

We can also note NVAR or "Non-Value Add Required" steps, that might include things like regulatory approvals or audits that don't add value but are necessary to perform.

Timing our Processes

We can display these value add (VA) and non-value add (NVA) steps with a process timing band. In a Value Stream Map, the timings for our NVA steps stand out on the peaks, and the timings for the VA steps stay in the valleys underneath our map, shown in Figure 10.

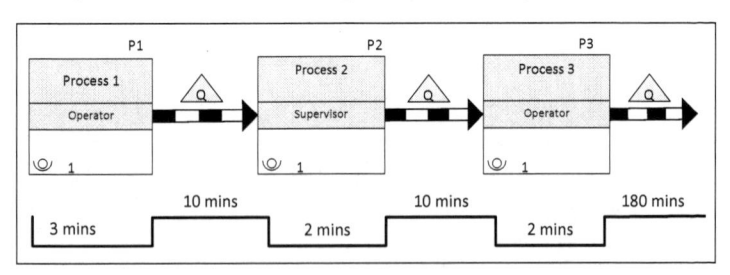

Figure 11: *An example of Value Add (process boxes) and Non-Value Add (queues) in a process map, shown by the timing band underneath each process. Value Add steps are shown in the valleys, while Non-Value Add steps stand out on the peaks.*

When gathering the timings for our process it is a good idea to time a process at least 10 times, then use the "lowest repeatable time" as the standard — the lowest time that appears three times or more. You may need to time more for fast processes and slightly less for slow processes, but 10 is often a good place to start.

There are also three main types of timings that we need to reveal:

1. Cycle Time, which is the time of a single process. This is noted underneath the process step.
2. Lead Time, which is the total time to create and deliver a product or service. This can be noted at the end.
3. Takt Time, which is the rate of items required as determined by the customer, for each shift.

To get our Takt time, we take the average items sold (or serviced) and divide it by the hours worked. For example if Lisa's customers called through 40 times a day (per operator) and she worked eight hours (480 minutes), her customer demand would be one every 12 minutes (480 minutes, divided by 40 calls = 12 minutes a call).

Of course, all of these timings relate to "Delivery" in our Customer Driven Metrics (1.2). Now that we have all this information, let's add it to our Value Stream Map and see what it looks like:

FIVE MINUTE LEAN

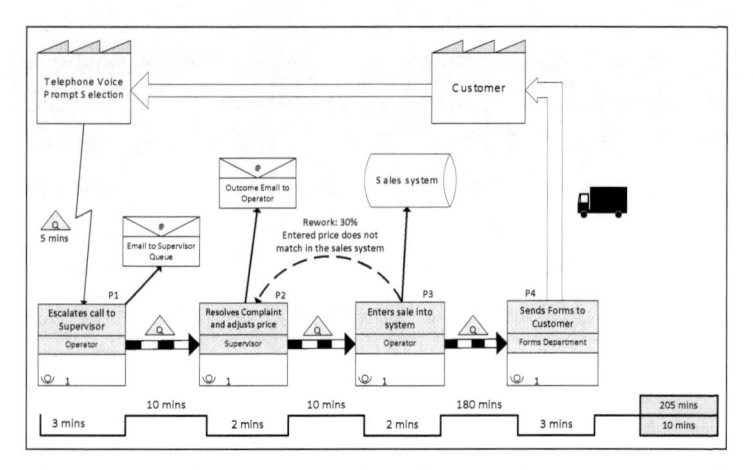

Figure 12: *A Value Stream Map of our Shoe Emporium process, now with rework, process timing separated into Value Add and Non-Value Add as well as the other common icons. The Takt time can be added separately.*

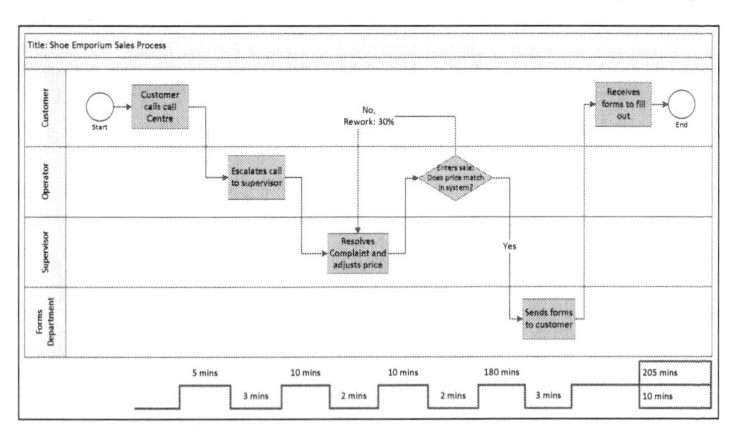

Figure 13: *A Swim Lane Flow Chart of our Shoe Emporium process. Although it is uncommon for a map like this, the important NVA times (the top times) and VA times (the bottom times) are also noted, with the totals on the right.*

So well done! There is a lot to take in in this chapter, but you did it.

On your journey you will notice that different people and organisations might lay out their maps slightly differently. As long as there is an agreed standard within your company, then including the information listed in this chapter at a minimum will give you enough insight to start making improvements.

If you are doing all of this for the first time, it can be a truly eye-opening experience. There might have been something that annoyed you in your job or business that you just couldn't put your finger on — but when you map it all out you can actually *see* it. You can see where the hold ups are, the rework, bottlenecks in the process and more. It's amazing, and it can really improve your work and your life.

3
REDUCE WASTEFUL STEPS AND IMPROVE FLOW

Where Lisa Performs a Balancing Act

At the call centre for the Shoe Emporium, Lisa got in extra early for her shift. There was no taking any chances today — she didn't know if there would be any more crazy announcements, and she definitely didn't want a repeat of the other day. The last thing Lisa needed was to give Robert the Boss an excuse to make her last three weeks here more miserable than they were already.

Lisa dialled in to her phone, looked at the phone queue and got ready for the onslaught of calls.

"Hello Lisa, guess who?" said a rather cheery voice in her ear.

"Oh my God!" she jumped up from her chair, nearly spilling her coffee over the desk. "Steve, how in the world did you get on the other end of my phone?"

There was laughter on the other end, and Lisa took a moment to compose herself. "That's not funny!" she added.

Steve replied between chuckles. "I called your service number and had one of your team-mates put me through to you," he said. "Did you know it took me five minutes just to press all the options and get on to a real person?"

"I know," groaned Lisa. "Believe me, I hear it from my actual paying customers every day," she added, with a grin.

"I'll be quick, I promise," said Steve, taking the hint. "There's some stuff I really need to tell you to help you on your journey, especially as you're running out of time."

Lisa grabbed a notebook and looked around the office to see if anyone had noticed her unusual antics.

Steve continued. "Yesterday I noticed your office kitchen bin was overflowing. In fact, there was a lot of extra waste in it."

Lisa looked over her shoulder to the kitchen bin. It was still unemptied, a few flies had made it their home and it was starting to smell. Yuck, she thought.

"Yes, and there still is," she confirmed.

"Perfect, because that's exactly what has happened in the company you work for," continued Steve. "Each process you perform for your customers has so much extra waste in it that it's becoming unpleasant for them to stick around any longer. They have no choice but to leave and shop elsewhere."

"What are you saying, our process is like last night's leftovers?" said Lisa half joking, half trying to understand.

"It's a different kind of waste," said Steve. "There are eight types of waste you see in businesses every day. But the most common ones for your business are having to redo work, waiting on work from other processes, navigating uneven workloads and having too many non-value added process steps."

Lisa was writing furiously as Steve spoke.

"So think about those things when you do your first Map. Especially, make sure you add in timings of your process and things that don't add value to your customer, like queues or wait time. You can use these to reduce that wait time later on. When you add them all in you can see where you need to improve."

"Steve, I love talking to you, but sometimes our conversations make my head feel like it's about to explode."

Steve laughed. "I know it can be a lot to take in. Maybe you could use a little sugar-hit? Look around your desk."

Lisa looked to the side of her desk and there was a box of donuts, fresh from the boardwalk. She looked around the call centre and her friend Jerry gave her an enthusiastic wave.

"Steve, how did you…?"

"It's amazing what your colleagues will do with a little bribery," said Steve, obviously glad his ploy had worked. "Jerry, I think his name was?

"But I got those for you for another reason. Notice how each of those donuts is labelled clearly and separated into its own section within that box?"

Lisa opened the lid, and sure enough the layout was immaculate. Each flavour had a clear label and a separate spot, appearing to be much nicer than donuts from a regular store.

"When you are reducing the eight wastes, a good place to start is with a thing called 'Five S' to organise your workplace, just like that donut box. Five S is where we Sort out any unnecessary items, Straighten and arrange them so they are easy to reach and have a clear, visible home, Shine and tidy regularly, ensure it becomes the new Standard with labels and clear outlines and then Sustain it by redoing it regularly."

"Very clever Steve," said Lisa. "Sort, Straighten, Shine, Standardise and Sustain. I can think of a few places I might use Five S already. And just so you know, I am going to use those donuts. Jerry is about to have lunch, and I know if he helps me with the map, then others will come and help too."

"Perfect!" said Steve warmly. "Now I'd better go. We wouldn't want to get old red-face involved again."

Lisa laughed. "Goodbye Steve."

She looked over at Jerry and picked up her box of donuts. Jerry smiled, and gave a longing look at the beautiful box — it seemed as though in bringing them to her he had gotten a taste, and he wouldn't take much convincing after all.

It was time for them to make a map.

※ ※ ※

Half an hour later, with two more friends Anne and Ron who agreed to help in return for a donut or two, Jerry and Lisa had mapped out their process over lunch. In fact, while they had been sceptical at first, there was a definite buzz in the air as they left the meeting room with a rough Value Stream Map firmly in hand.

"I can actually see the process!" said Jerry, waving his hands around excitedly. "The delays and rework, why it is so frustrating, everything!"

Even Lisa was chuffed. They had found a few process steps that weren't really necessary and could be combined to help make the process faster.

But as they spoke excitedly and walked back to their desks, they were interrupted by a loud, grating voice.

"Does the name Sarah Stephenson ring any bells to you?" It was Robert the Boss, his red face creased in a frown, and Jerry, Anne and Ron suddenly made themselves scarce. Lisa looked up at Robert and nodded, but remained silent.

"Her wedding shoe order from three weeks ago never arrived, and her wedding is tomorrow. Now she is asking for a refund that this company can't afford to make. This is your order Lisa. Fix it or it's coming out of your pay!"

Lisa's heart sank. She knew Sarah, she was her best customer. Lisa watched as the boss stormed off past the "outgoing items" department in the middle of the floor and groaned. Sorting through the items in that department to try and find Sarah's order would be like finding a needle in a haystack — the place was truly a mess. This was not going to be easy.

"Robert, wait!" Lisa called and hurried after him.

"Maybe I have something that can help. My customers told me that they want overnight shipping. If we brought this in perhaps we could use it to get Sarah's shoes to her in time?"

Robert looked back at her sceptically, but said nothing, so Lisa continued.

"They also said they'd be willing to pay more for our niche brands and longer return periods as VIP customers. I was thinking, these are all things that could give the call centre more time."

Robert was silent for a moment.

"OK," he said in his gruff voice, "but don't think this lets you off the hook. I still want that order found!" And he stormed back into his office. Lisa breathed a sigh of relief. It was time for some fresh air.

❂ ❂ ❂

Stepping out onto the boardwalk, Lisa felt it had been a busy morning already. As hard as she worked on the Lean tools she was learning, sometimes it still seemed as though there was a long way to go.

"Nice day for a walk, isn't it?" A familiar mop of light brown hair was warming himself on a park bench in the sun.

"Steve! I should have known you'd be here," and even though she was relived, she added, "Don't you ever do any work?" and grinned.

"With the good standard processes I have in place, Lisa, I don't have to," Steve countered. "My employees have everything they need.

"How did you enjoy the donuts?" he asked.

"They were great, Steve. In fact my team-mates ended up enjoying helping out — we even found a few processes we can combine to get rid of queues and wait time."

"That's great, Lisa!" Steve smiled. "I was actually just passing through, but I did want to show you something while I'm here. Look at this." He motioned across the boardwalk and leaned in so he could talk quietly.

A young girl and her mother were having a "discussion" near the ice-cream stand, although discussion was hardly the right word. For every time the mother told her child that she couldn't have an ice-cream, the young girl simply asked "why". Over and over and over again.

"Kids sure are persistent," noted Lisa.

"And that girl is asking the right question," said Steve. "In our business, if we want to get to the real reason behind something we ask "Why?", and we continue to ask it until we get to the root cause of the issue. I think you'll need that in the next few days, as you run into problems in your process that you need to fix, and try to define it properly with your team-mates."

Lisa nodded. "I think I will too. And it looks like "why" is either going to get that young girl an answer, or an ice-cream," she laughed.

"Exactly," said Steve.

Lisa turned towards her building. "Thanks, Steve. I'm glad you're here," she said. But now, it was time to get back to work.

✿ ✿ ✿

There was a large commotion on the call centre floor as Lisa made her way back to her desk. Many of the call centre employees had gathered, and in front of them was Robert the Boss, microphone in hand, already speaking to the crowd.

"...So that is why I recently came up with the idea of overnight shipping on items, and up-selling the niche brands that our customers have grown to love. Because of this, the board of directors have decided to put off the closing of our call centre by one week. Thanks to me, we just might have a chance."

There was applause and relief from the crowd, but Lisa couldn't believe what she'd heard. Did he just say *he* came up with those ideas? The ideas that she had literally only given him a short while earlier? Lisa's fists clenched together, her nails digging into her skin as Robert the Boss finished off his speech to more applause from her team-mates.

As the crowd dispersed, Robert lingered a little and caught her eye. He flashed a knowing smile at Lisa before turning around, and disappeared back into his glass office.

Sitting down in stunned silence, Lisa looked over at Anne to find some support. Anne saw her, but her eyes widened, and she looked away.

That's strange, thought Lisa.

She looked over at Jerry and gave him a small wave. But Jerry pretended not to see her, staring straight ahead and then slouching so he was out of view.

Something was going on, she thought.

The rest of the afternoon was a blur to Lisa. It seemed as though her job, her ideas, and now even her team-mates were being taken away from her, but Lisa could still do what she did best.

The afternoon turned into evening, and Lisa took call after call, helping person after person with their varied needs around shoes. The more people she helped, the better she felt. By the time she hung up on her last call of the day, Lisa knew what she had to do.

If she was going to find Sarah's missing order, she would have to brave the outgoing mail area that looked like a bomb had hit it. Only now she had the perfect tool — the Five S that Steve had taught her. She was sure that if she tidied it up, used labels, marked areas and put things close at hand, she could also save the people who worked there many hours of work each day. Sort, Straighten, Shine, Standardise and Sustain.

It was dark outside and there was no one left on the floor as she had worked so late, and as she began sifting through the mountains of paper and boxes Robert the Boss came past as he left for the night.

"What are you still doing here?" he asked, genuinely surprised.

Lisa gritted her teeth. "Just doing more things for you to save the company with," she replied, with more than a hint of sarcasm in her voice.

"Yeah well, make sure you lock up on your way out," he said, and looking over his shoulder he added: "They're not going to keep this call centre, you know. That stuff about the board of directors, I was making that up. They're meeting in three weeks to decide whether to off-shore the rest of this company after this centre goes. It's just a matter of doing the numbers."

Lisa's anger grew. "What? Why would you tell me that? These people are counting on you, Robert!" she said, raising her voice.

"Because I know you would never do anything to hurt your beloved Shoe Emporium," replied Robert the Boss, with a goading grin. "Of all the people I could tell in this place, you are my safest bet."

And without another glance, he left.

Lisa kicked a few of the boxes out of her way in disgust, and they scattered in a pile around her. As she sat down and looked through the pile, a label caught her eye. It read:

"Sarah Stephenson: URGENT"

Oh my God, thought Lisa. It was the missing order! It had never even left the outgoing department, the place was so cluttered.

Lisa didn't know whether to laugh or cry — the whole process at the Shoe Emporium was obviously broken. At least now, with Robert using her idea of overnight shipping, she could make sure that Sarah got her shoes before her big day.

Robert the Boss' horrible attitude had only served to make her more determined. Lisa knew what she had to do, and with each passing day she was getting the tools to do it. She knew she could make a difference.

What she didn't know was why her team-mates were acting so strangely. Although, she was about to find out, and when she did, it would turn everything she had done so far upside-down.

❂ ❂ ❂

3.1
Eliminate the Eight Wastes to Improve Flow

"The eight wastes are a standard, fast and easy method of discovering ways to make our job better."

Now we get to the really good stuff—in fact, this part is my favourite. The best thing about mapping our process in the previous step is that it makes it easy to see possible ways to improve. Articulating any wasteful steps or processes also helps us clearly define our problems before we begin.

At the Lean Enterprise Institute, this third step is called "Flow". As we go through step three you will see that reducing "waste" in our processes will improve how well and how quickly those processes flow from beginning to end.

The Eight Wastes are a standard way of identifying process blockages in a Lean transformation, and they form a wonderful acronym: "D.O.W.N.T.I.M.E." The Eight Wastes are:

1 **D**efects
2 **O**ver-production
3 **W**aiting
4 **N**on-effective use of time and talent
5 **T**ransport

6   **I**nventory
7   **M**otion
8   **E**xcessive processing

Let's find out what they mean below, and see if you can recognise any of these wastes in your own job, company or processes (here's a hint: you definitely will).

Defects (and rework)
Defects are mistakes that require rectification, including rework; or worse, an item being scrapped completely. This might include a job not done properly the first time that needs to be re-done, or items that can't be delivered because they don't work as they should. The cost of team-mates time and resources to perform this rework can be staggering.

Over-Production
Over-production is producing more of our goods or services than necessary, and that do not meet the specific needs of our customers. Ideally we will produce items only when our customer requests it, with a small buffer of items to meet demand if necessary.

Waiting
The waste of Waiting is when groups of team-mates in downstream processes are waiting for the completion of upstream work. Have you (or your customer) ever waited

too long for someone before you (upstream) to complete their work, while you were unable to do anything?

Non-effective use of time and talent

This is the failure to fully utilise the time and talents of employees. It will include things like not using the front-line process or customer expertise of staff, or not asking for input in solving problems from relevant team-mates who are experts in the process they perform.

Transport

The waste of transport relates to unnecessary transport of material, items in production, information or products. For example, a warehouse that shifts things around too many times, or worse still — moves items from manufacturing, to a warehouse, then back to manufacturing. Or in an office environment — moving things between too many systems, folders, forms or departments.

Inventory

This waste refers to the production of inventory that no one wants (or has requested). It costs money and time to produce and store items, and companies often have additional inventory lying around because they can't yet produce at the rate of customer demand. The more inventory, the costlier it is.

Motion
This is unnecessary movement by employees active in a process. Reaching too far, moving around to get to things or, in a technology environment, having to sort through items, or folders or systems to find what you want, all relate to motion.

Excessive Processing
This means processing steps that are not needed, or any steps that don't add value to the customer. This could be excessive approval steps, meetings with no outcomes, or anything else that does not specifically add customer value.

Two additional inefficiencies that are noted in Lean are also:

Overburden:
Unnecessary burden or stress on people or equipment, often because of waste.

Unevenness:
Peaks and valleys in workloads creating too much idle time, followed by times of stress.

Can you see any of these in your own company? How about examples in other jobs you've worked in?

One of the most important wastes to note during a Lean transformation is number four — failing to utilise the time and talents of people. For a transformation to happen quickly and with enough momentum, it must be taught to all levels, including management or owners who can properly support a change initiative, and front-line staff who know their customers and the process well and can share valuable knowledge on how to improve it. This ensures that everyone is on the same page, speaking the same language, and can use the same problem solving tools in combination with their own process expertise.

Most people can see at least one of the eight wastes in their own work, and many will be able to see four or five.

Note them into your Value Stream Map as Kaizen Bursts (2.5) so you don't forget them.

3.2

Use Pareto to Find Where to Start

"The 80/20 rule states that 80 percent of our problems or opportunities come from 20 percent of the inputs. A Pareto chart makes it easy to see where our best opportunities are."

In some cases we might have a few different problems to choose from when improving our job or business. When there is more than one option it can be a good idea to discover the area that will give us the most value for our effort and start there.

Pareto Analysis or the "80/20 Rule" is a tool that can help us discover this, and quickly. The theory is that 80% of our results often come from 20% of our effort. This is the kind of thing Steve might point out at the boardwalk, where a restaurant might make 80% of its profits from just 20% of its menu. For Lisa it might be that the Call Centre loses 80% of customers waiting in queue because one of the five voice menu options sends them to the wrong place.

The amounts don't have to be exactly 80/20, but you will usually find one or two stand out processes or problems that can give you a larger return on your effort if you focus on it first.

A Pareto Chart is a bar chart of whatever we are measuring — whether they are queue times, number of requests, sales figures, defects or mistakes. This bar chart is sorted from largest to smallest, and a line chart is then placed over the top of it showing the cumulative percentage as it grows from 0% of the results to 100%. In this way we can see where our larger opportunities are (such as in the first two queues in Figure 14) as they make up the majority of around 70% of the total time, and we can focus on these first.

Customer Queue Time
Pareto Analysis

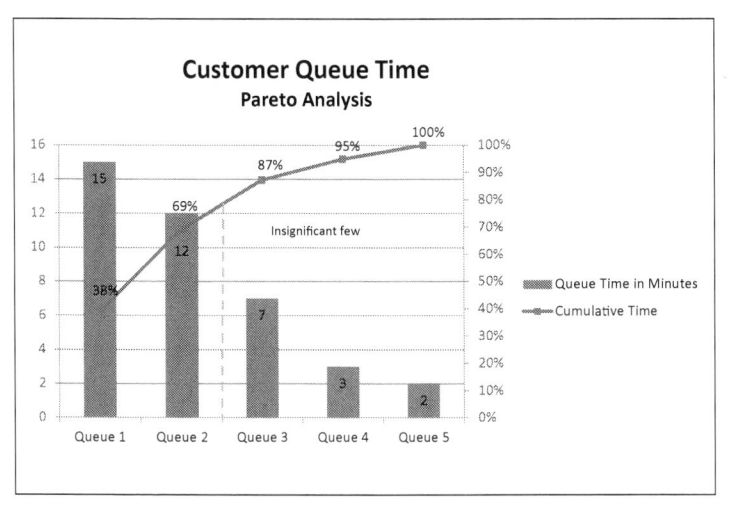

Figure 14: An example of Pareto Analysis. Queue 1 and Queue 2 have the longest times and combined they make up around 70% of the total — the "significant many". We can see that it might be valuable to start working on Queue 1 and 2 processes first.

By using a Pareto Chart, we can focus on where our biggest impacts might be. It is a tool that can be used for almost any input or when making a decision on where to start.

3.3

Solve the Real Cause of the Problem

"Using a Fishbone diagram and the 5 Whys is a fast and easy way to get to, and solve, the real cause of a problem."

Implementing solutions to problems in our job or business often takes time and money to do. Many people spend this time and money only to discover they were solving the wrong thing — addressing only the symptoms and not the actual cause. Using the power of Root Cause Analysis can help us discover and solve the real problem and avoid this waste. Problems are also wonderful opportunities — if we can solve the real problem it can make our job easier and far more enjoyable.

When we have a specific problem that we need to solve, it is extremely important that we:

- Clearly define the problem we are working on, before we begin.

This means we "go and see" the problem, directly where the work is done (at the Gemba, 2.2) and hopefully as soon as it happens (with Jidoka, 4.2).

It also means articulating the problem specifically as a gap from where we are to where we want to be, based on something measurable like our customer driven metrics

(Quality, Delivery, Cost or Sales, 1.2) or reducing one or more of the eight wastes (3.1).

For Lisa this might mean reducing wait time in a queue from 10 minutes (where she is) to five minutes (where she wants to be) instead of just saying "less queue time". Defining a problem in this way also makes it easy to know when you have succeeded — you are not chasing a vague concept. And because you have defined the problem as a measurable gap, it is also easier to present a clear view from the problem, to a solution.

During our Kaizen meetings, while mapping our process, or even when walking the Gemba, we may need to get to the real cause of these problems we reveal. To do so we use a Fishbone diagram and the "Five Whys".

Fishbone or Ishikawa Analysis

A Fishbone diagram is used to get a quick idea of *where* the cause of our problem might lie by separating ideas into categories.

The four categories are:

1. People
2. Information
3. Process
4. Systems

An easy way to remember them is "PIPS".

In Manufacturing, the four categories can also be known as the "Four M's": Man and woman, Materials, Method, or Machine.

To use a Fishbone diagram, Lisa would note her clearly defined problem at one end, the "head" of the fish. She could then have her team-mates call out reasons why they believe the problem is happening. These reasons would be noted under any of the four categories, depending on where the cause lies.

As usual, a picture says a thousand words:

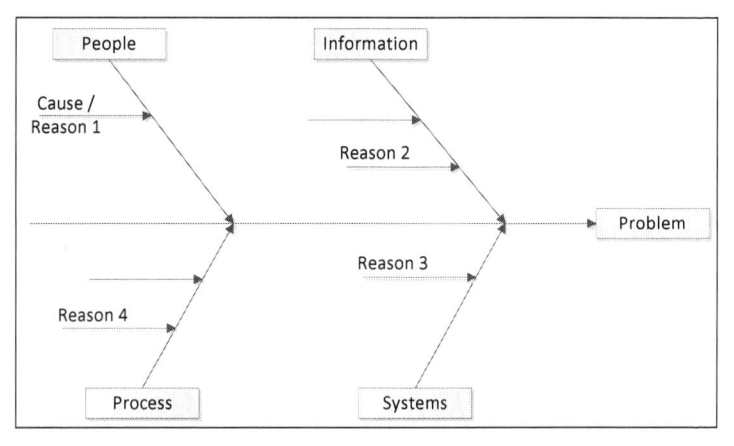

Figure 15: *An example of a Fishbone or Ishikawa diagram, noting reasons under People, Information, Process and Systems. Once complete, we can group similar problems or reasons together and then perform the Five Whys.*

Once she had a few reasons, Lisa could group them together further. For example, there might be a few reasons that relate to how people are trained, or others that always come back to a certain department. This allows her to narrow down her causes effectively into one or two main reasons, and she can then delve even deeper with the Five Whys.

The Five Whys

Once we have an idea of where our problem lies using a Fishbone diagram, we can use the Five Whys to delve deeper into any of the main reasons that we have come up with, if we need to.

To perform the Five Whys, we ask "Why" this is happening, and with each new answer ask why again until the answers have been exhausted or we need to gather more data.

Let's say that in one of the process steps at the Shoe Emporium Lisa identified that there is a high rework percentage, perhaps 50%. Maybe it's a form that doesn't get filled out correctly and needs to be re-done.

The conversation might go a little like this:

Why does the form come back for rework 50% of the time?
1   The customer doesn't fill it out correctly
Why?
2   They don't feel like they have to, or they don't understand it
Why?
3   We haven't explained the importance of the form or how to fill it out

Why?
4   We don't focus on building in quality when gathering the information, and it is too easy to make a mistake.

In this scenario we didn't need all five "whys" — this is OK. The main point is to keep asking until the answers have been exhausted, or we need more information. We also know our Five Whys are working when we can go back up the line of questions and replace "Why" with "Therefore".

For example:
4   We don't focus on building in quality when gathering information

Therefore:
3   We haven't explained the importance of the form or how to fill it out

Therefore:
2   Our customers don't understand it

Therefore:
1   Our customer doesn't fill it out correctly and it comes back 50% of the time.

Once you have narrowed down your answers, you can add the real problems into your Value Stream Map as Kaizen Bursts, and brainstorm solutions with your team-mates.

When you are brainstorming solutions, you can use ideas from Chapters Three, Four and Five to help you. This will give you tools such as having a standard process, error proofing or stopping when a defect is found, working towards one-piece flow, then changing how people are measured or rewarded and making information, process steps, queue times or other things visible, which can all have a huge impact.

It is also a good idea to use the 5 Whys on our processes — as in "Why do we do this step?" In many cases a process may have been created long ago and things have changed or moved on, leaving the process unnecessary. If the only reason for doing something is because "this is the way it's always been done," then thank goodness you are going through a Lean transformation!

3.4

Help Your Process Flow with Line Balancing

"A Line Balancing chart shows you where you can combine or split processes, to save wait time, reduce hand-offs and ensure you meet customer demand, all at a glance."

Line balancing is where we improve Flow by balancing out the steps in our process, so that they are faster than the rate of customer demand, or Takt time. This can mean combining steps where possible to eliminate queues or wait time, or splitting steps into smaller parts so they can be performed more quickly than our customer demands. A Line Balancing Chart helps us visualise it so we can see where we can improve.

Lisa might use this once she has done her Value Stream Map (2.4) with timings, and wants to see if she can make the experience faster for the customer.

As usual, a picture is worth a thousand words — let's look at the process steps we started with in our SIPOC (2.3):

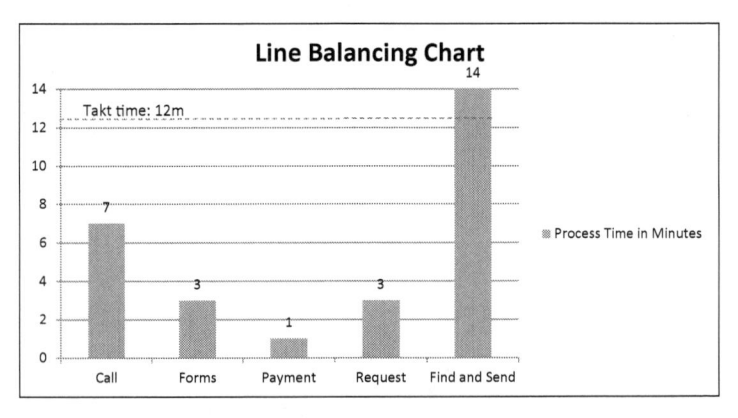

Figure 16: *Example of our initial line balancing chart, where each process step is being performed at the same time as they move along a "production line" that is always full.*

In the example above we have a service that needs to be produced once every 12 minutes to meet customer demand. In other words, 12 minutes is our Takt time.

To create this service, we have five process steps. Our timings look like this in minutes: 7, 3, 1, 3, 14. Every step is always working, as items constantly move through the creation process.

Our two longest processes are 7 minutes and 14 minutes each. We also have a problem, because if one step is taking 14 minutes and we need one every 12 minutes, we won't meet our customer demand.

So how do we balance this workflow?

We can see that the second longest process (step one, "Call") is 7 minutes. Steps two and three after it, however, only add up to four minutes (3 + 1). So we have the opportunity to combine the first three steps to reduce the number of total steps, with the added benefit of eliminating queues or wait time in between.

Step 5, however, is 14 minutes — 2 minutes over our Takt time. We can split this step into two, or add some of it to another step in order to bring it under 12 minutes.

Doing this and balancing out our process steps, we have a much more streamlined process with less wait time, fewer handoffs and that we know meets customer demand.

Line Balancing Chart

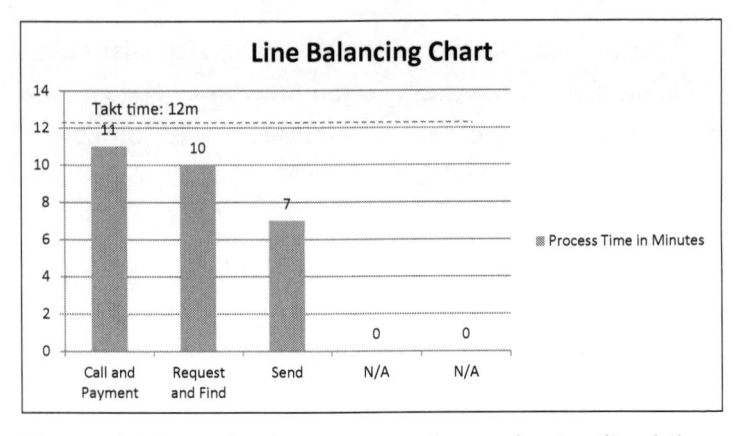

Step	Process Time in Minutes
Call and Payment	11
Request and Find	10
Send	7
N/A	0
N/A	0

Takt time: 12m

Figure 17: Example of our process after performing line balancing — some steps are combined, reducing queues in between, and one step is split up, ensuring our longest process is still under Takt time.

Using a Line Balancing Chart to Start Initiatives

Using a Line Balancing chart to start an improvement initiative is easy — we just need to reveal the right things.

Remember, when timing a process we do so a minimum of ten times and use the lowest repeating time (2.5). However, we can also draw in the *maximum* time for each step. This will show us the lowest repeatable time versus the maximum time, with the time between them revealing any variations in time when performing the process. And what causes these variations? You guessed it — waste (3.1) and not having or following a standard process (5.4). This variation can be a good opportunity to focus a Lean initiative on.

Reduce Wasteful Steps and Improve Flow

This is why problems are such great opportunities. Once the process is improved, we can create a new standard process based on the changes, and then improve it again.

Line Balancing Chart

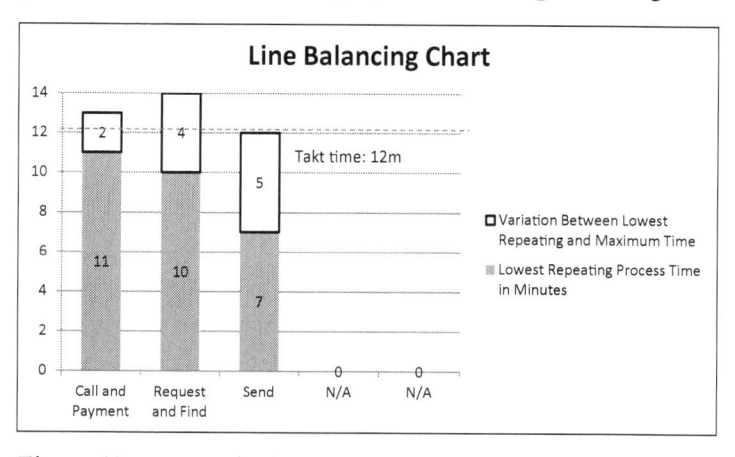

(Takt time: 12m)

Process	Lowest Repeating Process Time (minutes)	Variation Between Lowest Repeating and Maximum Time
Call and Payment	11	2
Request and Find	10	4
Send	7	5
N/A	0	
N/A	0	

Figure 18: *An example of a Line Balancing chart showing variation in times when performing a process. This variation is the perfect opportunity for a Lean improvement initiative.*

We could potentially reduce this variation and the time of any remaining steps as well. Getting rid of NVA steps or processes (2.5), getting rid of the Eight Wastes (3.1), using quick changeover techniques (3.5) or adding error proofing and Autonomation (4.2), using 5S to organise work-stations and keep items close at hand (4.4) can all help reduce and balance out our remaining total Lead time even further.

3.5

Work Towards One-Piece-Flow (and Reducing Silos or Batching)

"One Piece Flow allows us to create our product or service smoothly and to customer demand, one piece at a time, reducing inventory, queues and work in process."

One Piece Flow is where, instead of many different departments or processes creating large amounts of material or work, it is done in as close to the one place and at the same time as possible.

It also means that our product moves from step to step continuously, one piece at a time and with no build-up of work in between. In our Line Balancing example (3.4) there would always be one piece (and only one piece) working for each step, and those steps would be balanced to customer demand (Takt time).

One of the main ideas behind this is that by only working on one piece at a time until completion, if anything stops or holds up the process it becomes very clear, as the process simply cannot continue. It reveals problems, which is good as they are opportunities for us to improve, and we can then look at these problems as they arise instead of pushing them aside for later.

Performing the work in the same place and time, whether it is a physical space or using a single computer program, significantly reduces wait time between processes, reduces unnecessary people or tasks, saves on space, machines and resources and gives an opportunity for simpler management.

One piece flow is also opposed to "batch processing", where items build up in a process causing larger inventories, longer queue times and rework.

Many of the eight wastes (3.1) will affect one piece flow. Unnecessary movement, transport, additional process steps or unevenness in a process can all slow things down. We can use our value stream map to see some of this waste, then root cause analysis to get to the real problem, and Line Balancing to see any variation in timings and balance the process to customer demand.

A Pull system, including Supermarkets and FIFO lanes and Kanban triggers in the next chapter (4.1) can also greatly assist with implementing one piece flow. Before we finish this chapter let's look at one last thing:

SMED and Quick Changeovers

Just a quick note on Single Minute Exchange of Dies (SMED), which is another way of saying "quick changeover" techniques. Sometimes our process might have long wait times as we change between processes, people, machines, systems or tools.

While it is easy to see how a quick changeover can apply to a manufacturing machine creating two different items, it can apply to an office environment in the form of changing between people or processes as well. Brainstorming ways to change over quickly, based on the instructions below can help reduce this wait time.

The method for quick changeovers is based on two types of changeover operations which should be separated from each other:

- Internal, or "hidden" operations, which can only be done separately and when the person, process or machine is stopped, and;
- External, or "visible" operations, which can be done in parallel while the person, process or machine is still going.

The aim is to reduce any waste (3.1) in the changeover, and then to:

- Convert any Internal (hidden) changeover operations to External (visible) changeover operations.
- Perform these changeover steps in parallel to each other (at the same time) or while the process is still running.

Can a client's details be filled out by someone, in parallel, while they are having their consultation? Or could a person changing roles within an organisation complete some of the changes themselves by making an internal, or hidden process, external and accessible? With a little imagination, we can transform our job and make it easier, which is why our first step would always be to "go and see" at the Gemba. Front-line team-mates often have great ideas on how to make hidden processes visible and complete changeover steps in parallel.

By putting all the steps in this chapter together we are reducing blockages, wait time, employee and customer confusion and unnecessary steps. Just doing this alone has the potential to add massive value to your company, department or business, and there are still more ways in the last two chapters to help you improve your work even further.

4

USE A PULL SYSTEM AND BUILD IN QUALITY

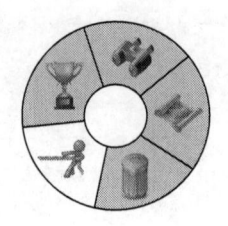

Where Lisa Pulls the Trigger

Something strange was going on at the Shoe Emporium. Lisa had barely seen Anne, Jerry or Ron ever since they had mapped out their process and found so many places for improvement. If she didn't know better she would have thought they were avoiding her.

But now they were all seated together at the coffee station, and Lisa took a deep breath and walked down to see them.

"Hi Jerry, hi Anne and Ron," said Lisa, mustering the biggest smile she could as she approached.

Jerry looked around hesitantly. Realising they couldn't just leave, Jerry, Anne and Ron simply stopped what they were doing and stared wide eyed in her direction.

"Guys — have I done something wrong?" Lisa asked. "We were making so much progress. If we kept at it I know we could make a huge difference here."

Jerry slumped a little as he spoke. "We're not supposed to be talking to you, Lisa. It's Robert. A few days ago he sent us an email saying that if he ever caught us trying to help you again, he would fire us on the spot."

Lisa's jaw dropped slightly as she looked at Jerry, stunned. "Robert did that?" she said. She had expected bad things from Robert the Boss, but even this seemed a little too much.

Jerry looked away. "I need this job, Lisa. I wish we could help, but..."

And with that they walked away, leaving Lisa alone.

Making her way back to her desk, Lisa thought hard about what she could do next. She had come so far already — fixing up the outgoing department, mapping the Shoe Emporium process. But without her team-mates, she was stuck.

As she sat back into her chair Lisa felt someone standing next to her desk.

"Excuse me, but are you Lisa?"

Lisa looked up to see a well dressed woman in a skirt, shirt and suit jacket, neatly pressed and looking at her with a questioning look and a deep focus. She was quite obviously a woman of power. Despite her intensity, however, she gave Lisa a warm smile. Lisa instantly smiled back.

"Yes, I'm Lisa," she said, only slightly taken by surprise.

"Fabulous!" said the well-dressed lady. "I wanted to come and thank you personally."

Lisa could hardly think of what to say, so the well-dressed lady continued.

"I'm the manager for our incoming and outgoing items, and part of my team is the mail area over there."

She gestured to the mail area, which until a few days ago had looked like a disaster. Now, the space was neatly arranged, labelled, and it not only seemed more organised, it seemed calmer.

"The changes you made have had a huge impact on our team," said the lady. "I've been able to move three of my staff on to other duties and train them up to help in other areas. They are over the moon, but as well as that our orders have never come in and gone out faster. We're saving days at a time."

"Really?" said Lisa. "It helped you that much? But, how did you know it was me?"

"It's my job to know these things," said the lady, and she winked, adding:

"I see big things for you, Lisa. Keep this up, and you'll be telling me what to do someday. Assuming we don't all lose our jobs, of course." And with that, the well-dressed lady disappeared.

Lisa let out a deep breath, looked up at the ceiling and smiled. Finally, something had gone her way.

She pulled up her emails and immediately a new message appeared on screen.

It was from Steve, and it simply said: "Yacht club after work?"

The sun was warm on her skin as Lisa made her way down to the yacht club that afternoon. Looking around the entrance, she certainly felt out of place here, and underdressed. This was obviously a place for big earners — it looked like the place a CEO might hang out, not someone who worked in a call centre.

Thankfully, an energetic wave from across the entrance caught her eye, and she immediately felt more at home. Despite his zany sense of humour and sometimes ragged style, Steve seemed to fit into this environment as though he was born into it. Of course, Lisa knew that he had come from humble beginnings, much like where she was now.

"Hi Lisa! Are you ready for your next lesson? I chose this place especially," said Steve, bounding over.

"Lesson? And here I was thinking we were going to enjoy a nice meal," Lisa said with a smile.

"Oh, this is going to be much better, I promise. Besides, I can't stand the food here. Give me a burger and fries any day."

Steve handed his ticket to the valet who radioed for Steve's car to come around. While they were waiting another car pulled up — a beautiful red convertible — and two people who were just as beautiful got in and drove away.

"Do you see what's happening here?" asked Steve.

"What, you mean apart from the fact that everyone seems to be driving cars worth as much as my house?" joked Lisa.

"Well, apart from that. Dig a little deeper — it's to do with the process," Steve said, and continued:

"The cars only come around when they are needed. By giving this nice young man my ticket, I've triggered a call to action where they bring my car around. In other words, they deliver to me — their customer — only when I request it.

"Can you imagine what would happen if they kept bringing cars around, whether we asked for them or not?"

"Well, they'd have a build-up of unwanted cars," observed Lisa. "I think things would get pretty crazy around here pretty fast."

"Exactly," said Steve. "And here's the kicker — most businesses are run like a valet bringing cars without a ticket.

"They create product without customers requesting it because they can't make it on time and by request. And they push work onto the next people in the process, regardless of whether they are ready for it and regardless of how much of it piles up. And then everyone wonders why they have so much unused inventory left hanging around! All of this results in waste."

"And I've already seen first-hand how waste can ruin a company. I'm working in it," said Lisa.

"That's right," said Steve. "So by using the tools you've already learned, you can make a process work quickly and work towards a Pull System, where you only create product or move work at the request of your downstream customer."

The valet brought Steve's car around and offered him the keys.

"Now," said Steve as he got in and sat behind the wheel. "Feel like something to eat? I've got a craving for some French Fries."

"Count me in!" said Lisa.

It wasn't long before they were doing a very comfortable speed down the main road towards their local burger joint. As old friends, it was easy to hold a good conversation. The top was down and the wind in her hair gave Lisa a feeling of freedom.

"So I've been hearing some very disturbing things about your company," said Steve. "People are starting to talk as though it actually might not make it."

Lisa sighed uncomfortably. As hard as she wanted to believe that one person could make a difference, it truly seemed as though the odds were against her.

"It's true Steve. Robert the Boss told me a few days ago that what doesn't get closed down in the next two weeks will probably be sent off-shore. He said they are having one last meeting with the board of directors in two weeks' time to decide."

"Two weeks eh?" said Steve. "Hey look, I know things are hard for you right now. You've got problems with your team-mates, your job, but there are still a few more things we can do. As far as Lean tools go, we're just getting started."

Lisa looked over at her friend, but found it hard to shake her worried expression.

"Steve, you mentioned using a Pull System before. Is there more to it? I'm still not quite sure I understand it completely." These daily lessons were a lot to take in, but Lisa was determined to learn as much as possible.

"Of course," said Steve. "The idea is simply that we don't work on anything unless it is triggered by our downstream customer — whether it is the end customer or just the next "customer" of our process. The most common way to do it is with a Kanban signal. It's a signal sent to your supplier to say that you're ready for more product — often with the item details and amounts.

"Take this car for example. When the car needs more fuel, the fuel light goes on. This is a basic example of a Kanban — it is a signal given to me as the supplier, to replenish the fuel."

A look of clarity came over Lisa's face. "That actually makes a lot of sense!"

"I just came up with that," said Steve, looking pleased, and he paused for a moment as though he was filing it away in his memory so he could use it later. "But, while we're on it, there is something else in this car that I can show you.

"Do you see that USB port? Many cars have them these days, and many computers." Steve gestured to the dash.

"Of course," said Lisa.

"Well have you ever tried to put a different plug into a USB port?" continued Steve.

"No, that would be ridiculous, it simply wouldn't fit," said Lisa.

"Exactly!" smiled Steve, looking over but with one eye still on the road. "They have made it impossible to make a mistake. For us, we call this Error Proofing. You'd be surprised at how many things in your job you can change so that it is impossible to make a mistake, and the results are incredible."

"I can think of a few things already," said Lisa. "The payment forms our customers fill out often have mistakes on them, forcing us to call our customers back more than once. I know some companies have drop down boxes that make sure they only choose the options available to them to save them time."

"Yes!" said Steve. "There you go!"

"But Steve, if you're going to be teaching any more lessons this afternoon I am definitely going to need something to eat. A full head and an empty stomach is not a good combination."

"I agree, we're almost there," said Steve as he turned in to the burger drive-through. "I just love this place. Burger and fries?"

Lisa enthusiastically nodded her approval.

They ordered their meal and drove through to the pick-up window. Steve shifted in his seat and craned his neck to try and see inside. "This is just the best thing," he said.

"You must really like burgers, Steve," said Lisa, her stomach grumbling.

Steve got back into his seat. "I do, but I love their process of making burgers even more. These guys have stores all over the country, and you know what? The experience is the same no matter which store I visit. Hot, fresh food delivered quickly. Not only that, but almost the entire store is run by young men and women, often just out of school. How is it that these people can make such a world-class experience in their company?"

Despite her hunger, Lisa's brow furrowed in thought. "You know, Steve, I never thought about it like that," she said.

Steve continued. "The difference is that they have a single standard process that they teach and enforce throughout their company. Using this, it is done the same way every time. They also make things very visual. With the monitors, the beeps and alarms, it is fairly obvious if something is ready or is not working as it should, and everyone can do something about it. And what's more, the set timers for cooking each product are a great example of error proofing—it's almost impossible to get it wrong."

"Wow, Steve. I'm kinda glad we didn't eat at the yacht club now. This is really an experience." Lisa's mood brightened a little, and then brightened even more as the service staff brought their meal.

"Boy am I looking forward to this," she said and, before they had even driven away, she was digging into a freshly cooked burger and fries.

❁ ❁ ❁

It was late in the evening by the time Lisa walked through her door. It had been another long day of hard work and hard learning but, despite how draining it should have been, Lisa had never felt more alive.

In fact, she felt as though she was working towards something worthwhile. But the night wouldn't stop here. Lisa sat down at her computer, logged into her emails and began putting the finishing touches on her Value Stream Map. As she worked and checked through her emails there were two that caught her eye. One read:

> >From: Jerry, Anne, Ron
>
> >Subject: We'll do it. Count us in.

Lisa breathed a sigh of relief. They were willing to help! But at what cost, she didn't know. As long as Robert the Boss didn't find out, Lisa hoped they would be OK.

But the other email read:

"Robert: Important Information Regarding Your Job"

I can't imagine anything worse than another announcement, thought Lisa, and she clicked on the email from Robert the Boss.

But as the email opened and she began to read, Lisa realised something terrible. She looked at the contents of the email — and she read it again because it just couldn't be right. It was worse than an announcement, much worse.

Life at the Shoe Emporium was about to take a terrible turn.

✵ ✵ ✵

4.1
Create a Pull System with FIFO, Kanban Triggers and Visual Management

"By making our process visible, including visual triggers and a small standard inventory where necessary, we can create our product or service as our customer orders it, instead of working to create something that no one wants."

We know that our customer can be our end customer or anyone who is next in the process (downstream) from our department or process. In this part of our Lean journey we will start doing things to get rid of work piling up and being forced on us or our downstream customers.

At the Lean Enterprise Institute, this fourth step is simply called "Pull", and the idea is to create a Pull system as opposed to a Push system. What this means is that you or your department creates a product or service only as your customer (or downstream process) requests, or "Pulls" it. We don't "Push" our product to our downstream process or customer, or we don't create product unless it is asked for.

This has the effect of reducing large inventory of unnecessary items, reducing "work in process" or a build-up of unfinished work, streamlining the process and promoting one piece flow (3.5). This in turn improves upon our customer driven metrics of Quality, Delivery and Cost.

Many of the tools below will assist in promoting a Pull system, and fit nicely with the methods we've already learned.

FIFO Lane

FIFO stands for First in First out, and it is an outstanding way to make sure that stock doesn't go out of date, or that work is distributed fairly. It is most commonly used in a "FIFO Lane" where items in a lane are taken at one end and supplied from the other.

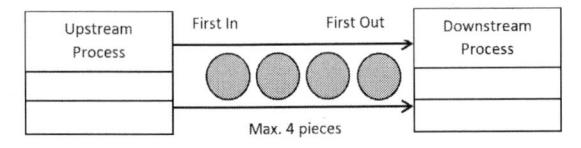

Figure 19: *An example of First In First Out — a small amount of inventory that takes the oldest first.*

You will have seen this in the bread aisle in your local supermarket — you take, or "Pull" bread from the bottom as you need it, and they restock it from the top. Of course, this is the best way to avoid stale old bread! But it might also be how you delegate work. It might be how you replenish perishable medicines. It might be the order in which you prepare food in after taking a customer's request in a drive-through. The main idea is that the item is pulled only as it is needed, and an empty space in the FIFO lane triggers the need for the item to be replaced.

Not every job will be able to create their product or process from scratch as quickly as a customer orders it. A bakery still has to bake their goods, and a hotel still has to prepare their rooms, for example. This is why keeping a small amount of "inventory" handy in any process via a FIFO Lane or Supermarket (below) can assist you in delivering quickly, without overproducing.

Supermarket

Another similar theme to FIFO is the Lean "Supermarket". A Supermarket is a predetermined standard inventory that is kept to supply the downstream process in exact amounts.

For example, if a doctor used 10 vials of medicine at a time in one operation, we might keep 10 of that particular medicine in one place so the doctor could take that exact amount for each operation. When that box is taken it will leave an empty space, triggering us to replace it with another pre-made box of 10.

Figure 20: A basic Pull system, where the customer pulls (orders) the product, and the empty squares prompt our team-mates to pull ingredients from their upstream supplier and create another product for the customer.

Kanban Trigger

Kanban is a Japanese term for "sign" or "signboard" and is basically a signalling system to trigger action. In other words, we ask ourselves:

- How do we know when we need to begin work on an item?

And:

- How do we let our supplier know we are pulling work (or product) so they can replenish or create their product as necessary?

What is the trigger that tells us these things? This is where a Kanban comes in.

Traditionally Kanban was associated with a "Kanban card", which was a card (or small "sign") holding details such as the product and quantity required of a product, handed to the upstream supplier to trigger production.

Time To Order!
Item: System Cards
Quantity: 5 boxes
Supplier : Stationary Co.
Please place this card in the plastic folder at Administration, and keep card 2 boxes from the bottom when replenished

Figure 21: A simple Kanban card, with standard instructions and quantities included.

In other industries, a Kanban can simply be any trigger to begin working on an item. It might be a green light telling us "ready to go!", it might be an "ORDER MORE" or "REPLACE" card placed where there are two left of something in stock, it might be an empty slot in a FIFO lane or an empty space (specially allocated by Five S in 4.4) for our Supermarket.

In a company using Agile techniques (5.3) it might be items in a Kanban "To Do" lane waiting on their wall. Ask yourself what the trigger is, or if you don't have one, what trigger would work best for you?

Visual Management

Visual management is another Lean method that can be applied to industries of all types. The idea is to increase transparency by making your process "visible". Things that are visible tend to get noticed, and things that are visible tend to get done. This can include detail of work queues, anything blocking the flow of the process, who is doing what or sizes of jobs; the list goes on and really depends on your industry or workplace.

For this step we ask ourselves:

- What information would be really useful to see at a glance, so we can know if things are working as they should?

Then we can go about putting this on one board, signal or sheet of paper for all to see. A Layered Check Act board (5.2) that shows process metrics is a good example of visual management. It could also be instructions for a process step made clearly visible at the work station with Five S (4.4). The Kanban board or Kanban card we mentioned earlier is also an example of visual management.

Visual Management is something that Lisa might use, if she wanted to make her sales calls visible. It is not uncommon for a call centre to have a large electronic board with the amount of people waiting, or the amount of people available to take calls.

If you come up with any ideas for visual management during your Kaizen meeting, add them to your current Value Stream Map as a Kaizen burst (2.5) so you can remember them for later.

4.2
Build in Quality with Error-Proofing and Autonomation

"By making it close to impossible to make a mistake, and making it easy to stop when something is wrong, we can save ourselves many hours in rework and many dollars of waste."

Using Error-Proofing

Poke Yoke is a Japanese term for "error proofing". The idea is to build in quality by providing constraints to prevent incorrect use, making it close to impossible to make a mistake.

An example of this would be a USB cable — you can only plug a USB cable into a USB port — nothing else will fit. It's mistake proof! This is Poka-Yoke. Another example would be the fact that many cars are unable to start if they are already in gear, or a form with specific drop-down menus so the user choice is limited, avoiding errors.

The question we ask ourselves for Poka-Yoke is:

- How do we provide constraints to prevent incorrect use in this product or process?

Figure 22: *An example of error proofing, where plugs around the home or workplace can only fit into the socket they are meant for.*

Using Autonomation

Autonomation or "Jidoka" in Japanese, means providing both team-mates and machines with the ability to detect when something is wrong and immediately stop work so they are not passing on defects to the customer.

Doing this also highlights any problems in a process, because work stops when a problem first occurs. By stopping when a problem first occurs, we can get a consensus on the root cause of the problem (3.3) before we try and solve it. Then we can put a quick fix in place at first to keep the process moving, and work on a long term fix directly afterwards.

Using an Andon, which is a light that shows the status of a process or operation (such as green for go, red for stop) is one way to use Jidoka.

The questions we ask ourselves for Autonomation or Jidoka are:

- How do we know when something is wrong?
- What is the visual signal we would like to see when this happens?

This step is an extremely important part of our ability to make problems visible (4.1) at the Gemba — Jidoka must be a part of each step in our process so defects are never passed through.

It is also one of the main principles of Lean that we "solve problems close in person, place and time", as they happen. To give you an example, let's think back to the Net Promoter Score in (1.3). If our customer gives us a six out of ten or lower, and we arrange to get this information straight away, we might call them to sort out any problem they might have right then and there, instead of letting it get lost in the system or losing valuable information from the source.

Implementing Jidoka with a Zero Tolerance for Rework

Jidoka is not just about stopping when we have a defect. At its core it is also about having a zero tolerance for defects and rework.

Before you implement Jidoka in your workplace, an easy way to begin is to have your team-mates set aside any item that comes to them requiring rework, and not work on it at all. Then, at the end of the shift, collect all the unfinished items and note down the different "defect" types. You can do a Pareto Analysis (3.2) to see which defect types are the most common, find out why they occur with root cause analysis (3.3), make errors visible if possible (4.1) and stop work if they ever happen again so you can fix them close to the source. This is Jidoka.

Add any Poke Yoke or Jidoka ideas that fit with your space to your current state Value Stream Map, as a Kaizen burst (2.5).

4.3

Level the Workload when Demand Fluctuates

"When demand for our product or service fluctuates, we can use Load Levelling, or "predictive Pull", to keep our workload level."

In a perfect world, we would know in advance what our orders or requests for service might be, so that we could have enough people or resources ready.

Unfortunately, in the real world, requests often come through in different amounts and at different times, with different items being requested. Most companies' response to this is to either constantly be behind in orders or requests (while their customer suffers), or constantly have too much inventory or people in a desperate effort to meet demand, creating all kinds of waste (3.1).

We have already seen how to balance the Cycle times of our process with Line Balancing (3.4), but we can also balance our workload when demand fluctuates using Load Levelling, or "Heijunka". By using information of *previous* orders (or demand), combined with information of *upcoming* orders (or demand), we can smooth things out considerably using the following techniques.

Let's say a company regularly receives orders, for any type of item or service, for 100 items a week, but demand fluctuates from day to day (for example 40 on Monday, 20 on Tuesday, 20 on Wednesday, 10 on Thursday and 10 on Friday), we could use a small buffer of finished goods (like a Supermarket, 4.1) to respond to Monday's high demand, then level production at 20 per day, meeting our 100 per week demand.

In Lisa's case, if call volumes at the Shoe Emporium fluctuate from day to day, Lisa might get this information by checking the historical volumes from the last week, month and year. She might recommend having more people working on a Monday (a buffer, like the example above) who would assist in smoothing demand.

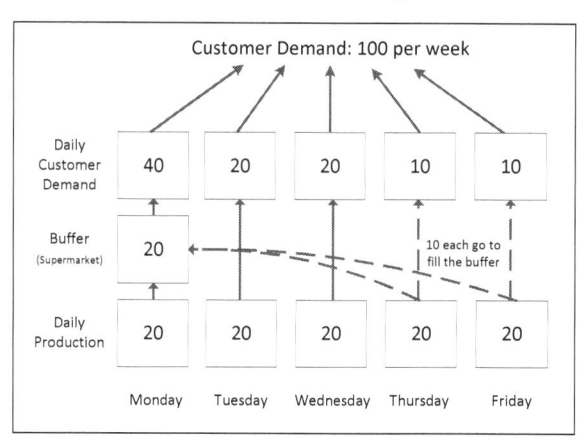

Figure 23: *An example of Load Levelling, where daily demand fluctuates. We can use a buffer, or "supermarket" on Monday to meet demand, then smooth production at 20 per day.*

Alternatively, we can also level the type of item we work on. Imagine a company has three types of products (products A, B and C), with daily demand being 20 for Product A, 10 for Product B and 5 for Product C, or a ratio of 4 : 2 : 1. Instead of simply lumping (or batching) the production of each item together at the same time or with the same operator, we can level it out so there is an even number being produced at all times, allowing us to respond to fluctuating demand more readily.

	Customer Demand A: 20 B: 10 C: 5 (4 : 2 : 1)
Batch Producer	A A A A A A A A A A A A A A
Lean Producer	A A B A A B C A A B A A B C

Figure 24: *An example of Load Levelling, where the types of requests are different. Producing the Lean way, especially when we have one piece flow, we ensure there is an even number being produced at all times.*

This is the type of thing that Lisa might use at the Shoe Emporium, if she got different types of sales and service requests by email. Instead of only one person performing one type of request, they can be spread across her team and ensure the requests are completed evenly instead of batching them together. This way there is less waiting while the one person completes their workload, and less chance of a single point of failure.

4.4
Organise Your Process with Five S

"Organising a workplace with Five S reduces risk, increases safety, makes it easy to reach and find things and know when they are running out."

In Lean, Five S (also "5S") is a method used to create an organised, clean and safe work area where things are visible, easy to reach and easy to find. This can also help in reducing waste, cycle times, overburden and stress and help implement your Pull system.

It doesn't just have to be a physical space either — in the world of technology it can mean reducing different and unnecessary programs, sorting out unnecessary fields in your software or forms, or reducing the many folders or areas we keep work, results, forms or code.

The five S' are:

1 ***Sort***
    Sort out and remove any unnecessary items.

2 ***Straighten***
    Organise the remaining essential items so team-mates can find materials quickly and reach them easily.

3 ***Shine***
    Clean the area and work tools.

4 ***Standardise***
   Make the standard process and the designated places for each item clearly visible for all to see.
5 ***Sustain***
   Put into place regular sorting and review of the necessary items and the implementation, for continuous improvement.

In other words, we have a place for our necessary things, and our necessary things in their place.

A nice example of 5S in a physical space is a "Shadow Board" — where shadows of the tools are put behind tools hanging on a wall so you know what goes where and can always see if something is missing. This idea can also relate to a Kanban trigger (4.1) to replenish an item. If the marked space is empty, this might trigger the upstream process to produce and place a new item there.

Item "footprints" are a similar idea — outlines and labels to show where items belong. All items should be close at hand, requiring minimal movement.

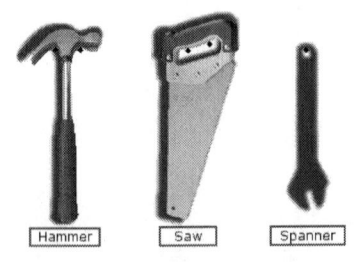

Figure 25: *An example of a shadow board, where the shadow behind the tool makes it easy to see what goes where, and when a tool is missing. Great visual management that can be seen at a glance.*

Implementing 5S

"Red tagging" items to begin our 5S is one of the easiest ways to start. We tag items with red tags or post it notes, and take them off if the item is used. This way it becomes clear if we have any items that we don't need, and can "Sort" them out. Doing a tally of how often fields are used in a software program (if at all) is another good way to tell if the field is truly necessary or not.

After we sort, "Straightening" an area can mean clear labels on storage boxes that help keep things in their proper place, and having items or tools within arm's reach so a team-mate doesn't have to move far to get them. This helps improve speed and quality.

When we want to "Standardise", it is also a great idea to show the standard process clearly on the wall of the area, making it visible for everyone to see (4.1). For example, you could place instructions for keeping an area clear or for storing things that come in, or the steps of the actual process performed in this area.

"Sustaining" a 5S effort is often done by making a roster clearly visible, with the date 5S was last performed and the date and name of the next person to perform it.

4.5

Put it Together With Design for Ease of Use

"The most successful companies have products that are easy for customers to use, and processes that are easy to create them with."

Design for Ease of Use (DFEU) is the idea that both our product and our process should be designed as simply as possible, so that anyone can use and understand it.

Truly, the more people that can use your product, the more opportunities you have to sell it. And the more employees that can perform your process, the easier it will be to find quality, capable staff.

It is no mistake that an average two year old can find their way around an Apple iPad, and that Apple as a result has been an immensely successful company.

This is why Design for Ease of Use is so very important.

The first step is asking our customer, "What is it you are trying to do?" The reason we ask, is because value is always determined by the customer (1.1). Whatever their answer is, we can ensure that our process gets them to that outcome more easily, by answering for ourselves the DFEU questions below:

1. How many steps are in the process? Can these steps be reduced?

2. Is Value added at each step?
   Can we remove non-value added steps?
3. How many wasteful activities take place at each step (3.1)?
   Can we remove this waste?
4. How long should each step take?
   Can we make them faster, and does it meet customer demand?
5. Why is the step necessary?
   What would happen if it was eliminated?
6. Are there any queues or stops?
   How long does the process stop for, and can we remove these queues?
7. What can go wrong at each step? Is it possible to make a mistake?
   Can we use Error Proofing (4.2) to avoid mistakes?
8. If the mistake cannot be prevented, can it be detected before it goes to the next step (4.2)?

And finally, the big one:

9. Would customers be willing to pay for this step if they knew about it?

To quote a phrase that is attributed to Albert Einstein—"Everything should be made as simple as possible, but not simpler." Making things easy to use is the pillar behind any great product.

5

IMPLEMENT WITH A STANDARD PROCESS AND IMPROVE AGAIN

Where Lisa Sets a New Standard

Lisa read over the email again, and felt her blood boil.

In fact, she had read it many times over the past few days just to make sure she had gotten it right. It was because of this email that she had been forced to work back an extra two hours every day, or risk losing her job when she needed it most.

Robert the Boss had seen her speaking with the manager of the outgoing department and somehow got permission from their CEO to offload some of his work on to her.

She read it again:

>From: Robert

>Subject: Important Information Regarding Your Job

"After speaking with our company CEO, and seeing as you obviously have time to chat with other managers, I am assigning you some additional work at his request. If you do not want to complete this work, I will take it as the tender of your resignation."

There was nothing she could do but stay back the extra hours each day to complete the work. Lisa couldn't lose her job, but she also couldn't continue to work there without making some positive changes, and the board of directors were meeting in a week to decide the fate of 300 employees.

A sudden thump snapped Lisa out of her thoughts as a pile of paper slammed onto her desk.

"Got time for a catch-up?" It was Jerry, standing next to her with a big smile on his face.

In fact, he had been smiling like this ever since he'd agreed to help on Lisa's journey. Everything they did now was based on trying to reduce the waste in their process, and the results were starting to show.

They would carefully form an idea for change, noting and minimising the risks using the tools Steve had taught them, then try the new method themselves and if the change worked they documented it. They felt like scientists, according to Jerry, and Lisa passed on all of Steve's lessons faithfully as he taught them.

Ron joined them as well, and Jerry continued:

"I worked on them all night, Lisa. I think this is it! I turned our changes into a standard checklist of things to do, so that anyone can follow it.

"And I also did the numbers—if everyone on the floor follows the process this way, we will cut our process time in *half*."

"Not to mention we could probably move two whole departments," added Anne, as she sidled up to Lisa's desk. "Did I hear somebody say "catch-up"?" she smiled.

Anne wasn't joking. The way they did their job now meant that they left out two whole departments — payments and customer forms — as they were able to complete these on the initial phone call. Even though changes like this were seriously above their pay-grade, they knew that based on the evidence they had gathered they could move those departments elsewhere, like sales or fulfilment, and bring much more value to the company.

It was beginning to be a typical type of meeting with Jerry, Anne and Ron, and Lisa smiled. They were actually glad to be at work.

"I'll take these down to see Steve now, guys. He can check it to make sure we're on the right track.

"I know it's not ideal, but once they're ready we will have to show them to Robert the Boss so we can try and save the company before next week's board meeting."

Jerry and Anne looked worried at this, but Lisa put on a brave face.

"I'll meet you back here soon."

She made for the elevator, pressed the button and waited.

As she did so there was a large commotion on the floor. People began to get up from their desks and move towards the common area. Not another announcement!

Lisa craned her neck to see. These things never seemed to be good news.

The people around her moved faster and started to yell.

"They're deciding today!" they said. "The shareholder meeting is today!"

Did she hear them correctly? The meeting can't be today, they weren't ready!

"I'm too late!" Lisa thought, and a terrible feeling washed over her as she realised that she could lose her job, and all that she had worked so hard for.

There must be something she could do. As Lisa struggled to think, there was a loud:

Ding!

The doors to the elevator opened, and standing to one side was a tall man, handsome and well-dressed apart from the fact that he looked like he had been awake for three days. His shirt was crinkled, and it was only 10 in the morning but he had a dark five o'clock shadow across his chin.

He held the elevator doors.

"Going down, or coming up?" said the man, managing a half smile.

Going down or coming up — that was it. Lisa realised she could go down the elevator, leave the building and never return to her job — or have no job to return to. Or she could go up the elevator to the board meeting with the documents she held in her hand, and do everything in her power to save the employees and the company.

Considering how far she'd come already, there was only one real choice.

"I'm going up," said Lisa, and the doors closed behind her.

As the elevator moved, the man leaned against the wall and sighed. He looked as though he was having a very bad day.

"Is … everything ok?" Lisa ventured cautiously.

"Let's just say it's been a long week, erm…" and he trailed off expectantly, waiting for a name.

"Lisa," said Lisa. "I work in the call centre."

The man seemed to do a double take.

"*You're* Lisa?" he said, looking up and brightening a little. Lisa was unsure of what to say, so she said nothing. "You're Lisa from the call centre, the one who has been making changes in my company?"

"Yes, I -" Hang on. Lisa's eyes widened. *His* company? Oh my God, thought Lisa, and her stomach turned. The nice suit, the lack of sleep before a major board meeting, it suddenly clicked.

This was Michael Pilbury, company CEO and the man she had once so admired in the early days of the business. By going up the elevator to the board meeting they had inadvertently chosen the same path.

"It was the only thing I could do. I've … been trying to save my job."

Michael Pilbury laughed a big, bellowing laugh. "So have I, Lisa-from-the-call-centre, so have I.

"I've been hearing a lot about you, Lisa," he continued. "People are starting to talk. I've heard about your group of high performers, and the changes you made to incoming and outgoing have made a huge difference to that department."

Michael thought for a moment, and then said:

"And even though your boss Robert has taken the credit for the new sales initiatives, I have a feeling they are related to the other changes you've made. Am I right?"

"That's right," said Lisa.

"Did you know that in the past week, your team has outperformed the others and sales have improved by ten percent? Ten percent, Lisa. That is huge! I wanted to ask, how did you do it?"

Lisa looked down at the small pile of papers in her hand.

"It's all in here," she said. "We were just about to finish them and show them to my boss in the hope that it could somehow save the company."

Michael looked sceptical.

"I wouldn't have too much faith in that approach, Lisa-from-the-call-centre, if Robert's past behaviour is anything to go by."

Lisa only nodded in response. He was right.

"I've got a meeting with the board of directors right now. They're not waiting until next week to decide the fate of my company; they want to close up shop today. Based on the changes you've made and the documents you have in your hand, I'd like to try and convince them to keep us here. No downsizing, no offshoring, just improved service and growth. What do you say?"

Lisa felt a sudden pang of doubt as she remembered: "They're not ready."

"But they *are* all we have," countered Michael.

There was no other way. Lisa handed over the documents. "There's an A3 summary of the whole thing on the front page," she said. "That will help."

The doors to the elevator opened. Michael stepped out to a large room with polished wooden floors and two large oak doors at one end. Lisa quickly reached out and held the lift.

"Wait — Michael, is this why you gave me all that extra work to do?" she asked.

Michael turned and looked over his shoulder. "I didn't give you any extra work Lisa," he said with a sympathetic smile, and with that the doors closed behind him leaving Lisa alone to digest what had just happened.

So, it wasn't him? That means Robert the Boss had lied. He had used the CEO as an excuse to get Lisa to do his dirty work, and Lisa had had no choice but to do it, or risk losing her job. She clenched her fists, half in anger and half in determination, and gave a silent vow to herself to somehow make things right.

Her entire future was now based on a prayer and some only just finished documents.

5.1

Create a Future State Value Stream Map

"When you can see a possible future next to a current reality you can see at a glance if your change is worthwhile."

Seeing the possible changes that can be made side by side with an existing process is one of the most eye-opening experiences ever. As a manager or business owner it is possible to lose touch with the ground-level processes, and seeing improvements mapped out clearly can be extremely valuable.

This step is called "Perfection" at the Lean Enterprise Institute, simply because when we are continually improving, testing changes and streamlining processes, then our aim of perfection becomes much more achievable.

Going through the steps so far, we have a *Current State* Value Stream Map that shows us our wastes, queues, rework and more. Once we have been through the process of brainstorming ideas for eliminating waste and increasing value, we need to show what it would look like in a *Future State* Value Stream Map and present it to the appropriate decision makers.

This is the kind of tool that Lisa can use to build a case and help management or stakeholders buy in to the change.

Have any existing processes been taken out? Have we taken out queues or combined two systems into one? Have we performed Line Balancing? Have we added in Supermarkets, FIFO, Error Proofing, Visual Management or new Kanban triggers? All of these will change the Value Stream Map, and now it's time to show the effects. We should ensure that our new reduced timings are included, including our new Value Add times versus Non Value Add times and the new total Lead time.

Presenting a change in this way ensures professional results, using solid data and facts to support them. An "A3" can also help your presentation, which we discuss in (5.2).

5.2

Present and Manage Your Change Using an A3 and LCA

"With an A3 "one-pager" you can see your entire project at a glance, with an LCA Board you can see your change's impact on frontline metrics at a glance, and with an Action Register you can keep everyone involved and accountable."

Remember Visual Management (4.1)? As well as being something we can use in a process (like Jidoka so we can see if a process is broken, a Kanban to trigger work or even organising with 5S) we can use Visual Management for our project and metrics. It all comes back to the question: "What information would be really useful to see at glance?"

Using an A3

An A3 is a "one-pager" that shows us the details of the Lean implementation quickly and simply — usually following the Seven Step Problem Solving process and with the following information:

1. The team and timeline (including stakeholders and facilitator)
2. Defining the problem
3. Analysis of the current situation
4. Root causes and proposed solutions
5. The action plan
6. Measuring the results against the baseline
7. The new standard procedure

Another way to put it is in the form of the most recognised Lean cycle — Plan, Do, Check, Act (and Adjust), as you can see in the example below. A good reason to start filling out your A3 straight away, is because the first step is "Define the problem" (3.3). Many people try to solve things without really knowing what the problem is — filling out an A3 first helps avoid this. You can then include things like your Value Stream Maps, any data collected, and root causes and countermeasures in your A3 as you progress.

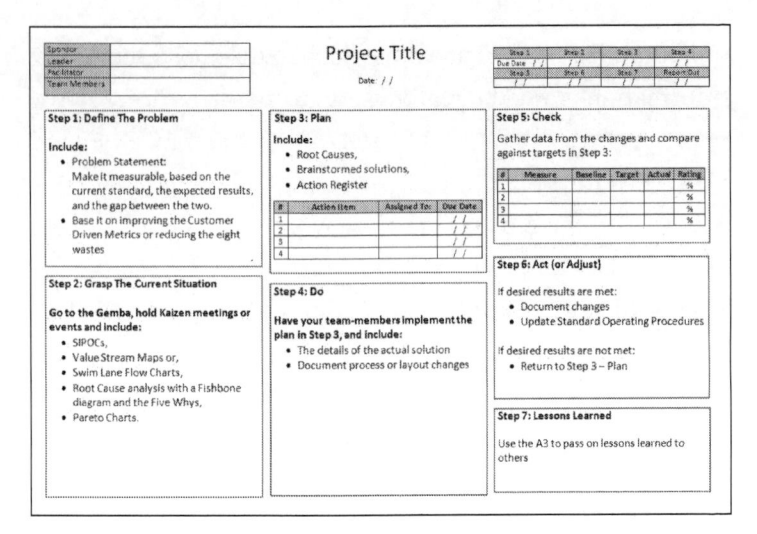

Figure 26: An example of an "A3", where you can see the details of your project at a glance, all on one page. An A3 template is included at the end of this book.

Another reason to start an A3 as soon as you begin, is that it helps you take your team-mates on the journey with you, and build their problem solving skills as well. They can see the steps outlined clearly in advance, and the techniques the team has used along the way.

Lisa would use an A3 to showcase the details of her change to others (like Michael Pilbury), and help take her team on the journey as they progress, passing on the tools and methods.

Using an Action Register

It is essential in any company to put the details of who will action each item during the implementation. This is

IMPLEMENT WITH A STANDARD PROCESS AND IMPROVE AGAIN

where an Action Register can come in handy, detailing changes, timeframes and who is responsible for getting them done. We should also include a "measure" of the item — with the existing data and the target data after the change is complete.

#	Action Item	Assigned to:	Due Date
1	Teach the A3 Seven Step problem solving method to the team	Lisa	/ /

Figure 27: An example of an action register. It is wise to assign action items, give them a due date, and make them measurable (Figure 28).

#	Measure	Baseline	Target	Actual	Rating
1	Teach the A3 Seven Step problem solving method to the team	0 people can teach it to others	8 people can teach it to others	8 people	100%

Figure 28: An example of a measures table that can be included with any actionable items, or in your "A3".

Giving team-mates responsibility for action items will help bring them on board for the change, and including a due date for completion will help keep everyone accountable.

Using a Layered Check Act (LCA) Board

A Layered Check Act board, on the other hand, is designed to display how a process is running. It will usually be at least one to two meters in length, and it shows the metrics of a current process measured against the proposed targets. This is great for seeing whether or not you are on the right track in your work. If the metrics are not meeting the proposed targets, then countermeasures are added, using Lean tools and methods, to assist in bringing them into line. For this reason, and as we come full circle, it is often a good idea to use an LCA board at the beginning of a Lean transformation, so you can see how you are tracking.

What metrics should we put on our LCA board? Ones that relate to our customer, such as Quality, Delivery or Cost, as described in (1.2). First Pass Yield, or Pareto charts on defect types are important metrics that relate to Quality. Lead time, Cycle times and Takt time relate to Delivery, and everything ultimately comes back to Cost.

There may also be internal things specific to your company that management wants to measure, such as having a standard process clearly visible for each step or station placed on your board. Remember, what you measure, tends to improve (5.5).

5.3

Implement With Agile for Fast Iterations and Feedback

"Structure everything as an experiment first. Agile is the perfect tool for releasing your change while keeping risk to a minimum."

Implement With a Standard Process and Improve Again

Agile is another methodology that can be used in conjunction with Lean to great effect, especially during implementation. It is primarily based on releasing things in short, quick "iterations", (implementations or experiments) to get feedback as quickly as possible. Iterations usually last from a few days to a few weeks before feedback is gathered, changes are made and the next iteration begins.

Additionally, we also want to release the changes we make in a controlled environment as a "pilot", where possible. For example, making changes on one machine instead of 50 machines, or with a small group of call centre consultants instead of the full floor.

Implementing in this way has many benefits. With no large rollout the risk is minimised. With faster feedback we are also getting rid of opinions and cutting through to the hard data—we can see if something is working or not. We don't have to put a lot of time and money into it to know if it works, and it also becomes easy to see if we have affected a downstream or upstream process adversely.

In Lean terminology this method of experimenting iteratively and gathering feedback is also called "Improvement Kata", and again relates to the "Plan, Do, Check, Act & Adjust" cycle. Using Agile simply gives that cycle a solid framework.

Prioritising a Backlog

The first step for the team, before an iteration begins, is to prioritise and display the work that must be completed during that iteration.

For example, team-mates would meet and write down all known and upcoming work (the "backlog"), put it in order of priority and place it on a card in the first lane of their Kanban board (below), giving them a "prioritised backlog". Doing this, team-mates can see what needs to be done for them to succeed. This backlog of work may evolve as new ideas or problems come to light.

Cards for a Kanban board are usually written as a story, for example: "As a _____, I want to _____," but they can also be in any format that is agreed within the team. In Steve's business, when he was improving it and making changes, he might write, "As a car cleaner, I want to have all my cleaning tools in one easy to reach location," for one particular change.

Using a Kanban Board

A Kanban board is used to show us at a glance the pieces of work and who they are assigned to as they move from "To Do", "In Progress", though to "Done". Remember Kanban literally means "signboard", and a Kanban board on a wall that is easy to see is also good Visual Management (4.1).

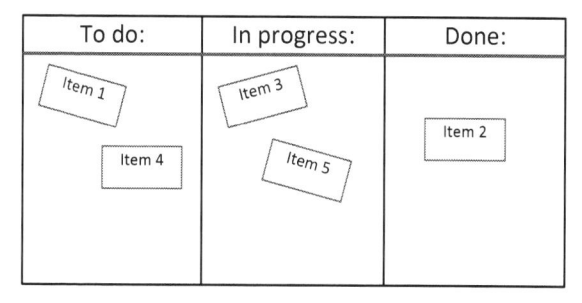

IMPLEMENT WITH A STANDARD PROCESS AND IMPROVE AGAIN

Figure 29: An example of a Kanban Board, also good Visual Management. This style of Kanban is often used in software development, but can also be used in implementing a Lean project or anywhere there are multiple tasks to complete.

You can have more columns if you need them, and name them to suit the phases of work or departments within your own business. The possibilities are up to you.

Using Stand-Ups

A "stand-up" in Agile terms is a short meeting of 5 to 15 minutes where the participants stand up, usually around a Kanban Board. Cards on the board are updated or moved as each person speaks about the ones assigned to them and they have the opportunity to raise any issues or "blockers" that might be stopping them from completing the work. If a blocker cannot be resolved within the short timeframe of the stand-up, then the decision is made to "take it offline", or discuss the issue afterward and make steps to solve it.

Standing up helps keep people focussed and the meetings short, and meeting regularly allows us to call out blockers close to when they first occur, so we can fix them close to the source. This is one of the principles behind Jidoka (4.2) and also one of the capabilities of outstanding leaders, which we saw in the introduction of this book.

At the Shoe Emporium, Lisa might catch up quickly, once a day with her team-mates who are trialling new methods, to see if they are working or if they need help.

Because we are releasing in short iterations, we don't have time for long meetings that happen once a month. Instead, we have short meetings daily, or weekly, and we can see all the information we need at a glance using the principle of Visual Management via the Kanban Board.

Using Retrospectives

A "retrospective" in Agile happens when we have completed an iteration. This is where our team asks the following four questions to gain feedback on our experiment.

1. What went well?
2. What didn't go well?
3. What have we learned?
4. What still puzzles us?

You might have many short iterations, named and numbered from one upwards, and it is great practice to stop and gather feedback during and after each one.

Knowing When it's Time to Pivot

One of the main themes from *The Lean Startup* by Eric Ries is knowing when to "pivot", or stop going down the path you are going during an implementation and pivot into a new direction, a new fix, experiment or even product. In other words, "Adjust"-ing our course in the Plan, Do, Check, Act and Adjust cycle.

How do we know if it is not working? If it's not immediately obvious in the experiment we are performing then we should measure the metrics or outputs (1.2) associated with the process or the product we are changing. As you can see, this brings us full circle as we go back to chapter one and gather feedback on whether we are meeting value as defined from our customer's point of view.

We can also ask the retrospective questions above for feedback on our internal process, or the Net Promoter Score (1.3) questions for our external customer.

When we are satisfied with our changes in a small area, we can release it to the wider business. And what do we do when we've improved our process and implemented successfully? We can monitor it and then go through the improvement process again as we strive continually for perfection.

5.4
Create a New Standard Procedure and Checklist for Quality Control

"When your process can be performed easily by someone straight off the street, then chances are you have an excellent Standard Operating Procedure."

And now finally we come to the point of it all! A standard, repeatable process that anyone can learn, teach to others, and quality check.

You will find that most businesses, even ones you have worked for, do not have clearly written, standard, repeatable processes for the work that they do. This means that the work is often "hidden", finishing very differently from person to person and relying on large amounts of expensive training, experience or even highly paid experts. Therefore, by simply articulating a standard process (making it visible) first, and then using the knowledge in this book to improve it, you can see some incredible rewards.

Taking our future state process and ensuring we have tested it well, we can now create a new Standard Operating Procedure (SOP) for people to carry out the same way every time, or use as a new baseline for future improvements.

The most common inclusions are a set of main tasks, and then sub tasks — simple step by step instructions from

Implement With a Standard Process and Improve Again

the beginning to the end of the process. A good process checklist will also include the takt time, or the rate required as per customer demand, the lowest repeatable cycle time (2.5), and relevant pictures, safety and risk notes.

When team-mates are using the same checklist as the person who is measuring their KPIs (Key Performance Indicators), then everyone is on the same page and their job is made that much better, easier and enjoyable. There is nothing worse than trying to do a good job while being judged or monitored on different rules (or rules that are always changing or are not clearly defined). This step truly has the power to fix these inconsistencies in an organisation.

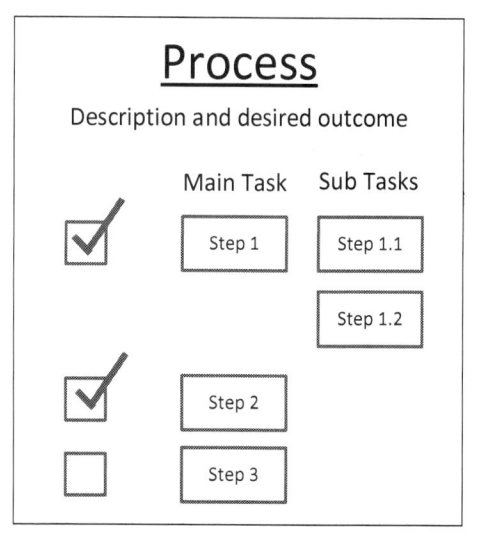

Figure 30: A checklist for your standard procedure doesn't have to be complicated. Keep it simple so anyone can create and follow it. Many people separate their SOPs into a handful of main tasks, and then sub tasks next to each related main task.

It's a good idea to keep your standard checklists in a central location where everybody has access to them, in addition to making them visible at the workstation and rolling them out to the people performing the process, the people training the process and the people monitoring the process.

5.5

The Power of Incentives — What is Measured and Rewarded Improves

"If you want to change how someone acts, change what you measure and reward to reflect it."

When you're effecting change in an organisation you should be aware of one of the most powerful influences of a person's behaviour:

Incentives — but it's not what you might think.

Billionaire Warren Buffett's business partner Charlie Munger famously said that he continually underestimates the power of a person's incentives. Think about the global financial crisis in 2008 — it was caused in large part by institutions financing thousands of terrible loans — simply because their incentives were married to how many they sold and not the quality of the loans themselves. Seems so simple now, doesn't it? But it made no difference to the salespeople if the loans went bad (which they eventually did), and it ended up causing widespread financial havoc.

So our last step when implementing a change in our company or organisation is this:

- To change how our team members work and act, change how they are measured and rewarded.

This doesn't have to mean monetary rewards either — it might simply be the difference between pleasure and pain in a task. If a task is extremely difficult or painful to do the right way, it subtly makes the incentive for our team-mates not to do it. If doing a task the wrong way is easier, the unspoken incentive is actually to do it that wrong way.

Changing what we measure has a similar result. If you want team members to stop passing on mistakes or unfinished products downstream (to the next step in the process), then stop measuring them by the amount they do and start measuring them on the quality instead. Make the focus on zero defects, and tie bonuses or Key Performance Indicators (KPIs) to quality or adherence to a standard process, with the amount they do as a secondary consideration. The same works for any other process output you are trying to change, in business and in life.

If you want better customer service, create a standard process around your customer service interactions then change what you measure and reward to reflect it.

Feedback (both good and bad) for these things is best given as soon as possible — the longer you wait the less powerful it becomes.

Understanding the effect of incentives on team-mates' every day decisions can truly change your business and your life.

Where Lisa Becomes a Leader

They had been in the boardroom under lock and key for over four hours — the highest paid people in the company undertaking a fierce debate on whether to close the call centre and offshore the other staff, or save the company and keep the jobs of 300 people.

The end of Lisa's shift for the day had come and gone, as had the clock-off time for every other person at the Shoe Emporium. But no one had left. They had all come to the boardroom floor to await the announcement of their future and their life.

Security had been called in to guard the doors in case the announcement went bad — although nearly all of the people already expected the worst. Then suddenly over the noise of the crowd, came the loud "click" of a door unlocking.

There was silence within a moment, and every eye turned towards the door. It creaked as it opened, and out walked Michael Pilbury, CEO, taking his place in front of the crowd.

There was not a sound in the room as Michael declined a microphone to speak from. He would deliver the news without it.

"Thank you for being here everyone," said Michael. "I've always known the people at the Shoe Emporium cared deeply about their jobs and the company, but now I can see it all with my own eyes." And he let out a deep sigh. The pause seemed to last forever.

"It is with deep regret..." Michael started, but the crowd, sensing the worst, erupted in collective outrage and his voice was drowned by the noise. Michael raised his hands and spoke in his deep resonant voice.

"Friends!" and the noise quietened. "It is with deep regret, that I announce the resignation of one of our senior board members, Alan."

Dead silence. Board member? Resignation?

"During our meeting today and based on some last minute information, the board has decided not only to postpone any offshore initiatives," Michael paused again for effect, "but also at this stage to keep every single staff member of the Shoe Emporium employed in this fine company! Yes there will be changes, and yes we have some work to do, but I believe that we can do it together."

And the crowd could contain itself no longer. Cheers and applause echoed through the floor, and didn't stop even as the board members filtered out from the room and into the crowd. Lisa caught the eye of Jerry, Anne and Ron and broke into a beaming smile. "It worked!" she shouted above the noise.

Team-mates were hugging as the news sank in, some were even crying tears of relief and joy as they realised what it meant for them. As nobody seemed to be leaving, pizza was soon ordered, bottles of champagne were bought and opened and the party really began.

But not everyone was in good spirits. Over the noise of the crowd bellowed a voice that Lisa had been trying to avoid.

"LISA! Did you finish that extra work I gave you to do?" Robert the Boss came storming into Lisa's space and got so close she could smell his awful breath. He took a hold of the pizza in Lisa's hand and shook it as he bellowed. "You don't get to enjoy this until you've finished your work, SO GET BACK TO IT."

Lisa stood her ground. She looked Robert the Boss in the eye, let go of the pizza he was shaking and got ready to tell him exactly what she thought. But she wasn't alone.

"I think you mean your work, Robert," it was the voice of Michael Pilbury, calmly but fiercely standing behind him.

"And she won't be taking orders from you anymore," he said. Lisa looked over at Michael in surprise. "In fact," he continued, "You won't have anything to do with this company at all. You are fired!"

Robert's face grew red. He opened and closed his mouth like a fish, but no words came out. Seeing that he had no allies here, he quickly ran out of the room. And that was the last time anyone saw Robert the Boss.

"Which means there is a space for someone to be promoted," said Michael, looking knowingly at Lisa.

"Do you mean me? I couldn't," said Lisa. "Michael I can't. I'm not a boss like Robert."

"That's right—you're not a boss, Lisa. You are a Leader. Despite your title you still managed to lead the people around you. The changes you've made and will continue to make have saved the jobs of over 300 of us here. Which is why I would be honoured and grateful if you continued to work on and improve this company in your new role as manager."

Lisa smiled. In fact, she couldn't think of anything she would rather do. "Well...if you put it that way," she smiled. "You can count me in."

Michael's face broke into a beaming smile.

"I was hoping your answer would be yes," said another familiar voice, and Lisa spotted a ragged mop of light brown hair bounding through the crowd.

"Steve?" Lisa nearly squealed with joy. "What on earth are you doing here?"

"I heard about what was happening, and came right over," said Steve.

"Steve happens to be a recent friend of mine," said Michael with a grin. "And he may have let it slip about some of the great things you've been doing," he added.

"It's amazing who you meet at the yacht club," said Steve. "Michael was very interested in what was happening at his company—very interested indeed. Sometimes it's easy to lose touch with the process, but with Lisa around somehow I don't think that will be a problem anymore." Steve smiled and looked at Michael, who nodded.

Lisa looked accusingly at Steve. "Why am I not surprised that you know my CEO?" she asked and then said half to herself, half to Michael, "Now I understand how you knew what I was trying to do here."

"That's right. And thanks to you Lisa, I feel as though we could get back to the old days, when it was about our passion for shoes and it was fun to come to work." It seemed as though now it would be impossible to wipe the smile from Michael's face.

Lisa nodded, and felt a swell of emotion and any words she wanted to say got caught in her throat. Tears started to well around her eyes.

"Thank you!" she said and threw her arms around the CEO. "And you!" she turned to Steve and gave him a hug.

Together they got another champagne, talked more about the way things could be and the impromptu party lasted long into the night. People discussed their jobs, their lives, and the changes they could make, and the futures that awaited them.

As the party raged on, Steve slipped quietly into the background and away into the night. He couldn't stay out too late — after all, he had a meeting with an old friend over lunch tomorrow who was having trouble with their job.

Steve chuckled to himself. It should be an interesting lunch.

Epilogue

So, you made it! Great job — the journey you've just been on takes many people months, even years, firstly to find this information then to learn and digest it. With this book as a Lean "standard process" in your hands, you should be able to explain to someone the steps around a Lean Transformation in under five minutes.

And there you have it — Five Minute Lean.

The power in this five minutes is huge. If you can describe something to someone in five minutes, you can convince someone to help you in five minutes. You can have someone on the same page as you in five minutes, you can attack any problems from the same side in five minutes. You can give everyone the same tools in your toolbox.

The benefit of Five Minute Lean is the ability to share it with all levels of a company, and do it quickly. Educating people gives you the momentum to ensure your transformation doesn't become just another "fad". Educating your team-mates allows them to rally around your cause instead of fighting, blocking or being indifferent to it through fear of change.

It increases the transparency of the operation and puts the "Aces in their Places" — where people performing the processes day-in and day-out have the mindset and the tools to improve their own working lives, their workstations and the company around them.

And lastly, it gives you the power of continuous improvement as you move towards perfection, turning the improvement process into a part of your culture so your team-mates can create their best life and work-life possible.

In fact, you might be surprised by the large number of people who take this on board once you explain it to them. When the improvements in your company start to flow and you help more and more people, then the rewards on your personal journey will flow even more greatly as well.

Yours in change,
Dave McLachlan

APPENDIX
Five Minute Lean Summary

Matched to the 7 Step Problem Solving Process	Step 1: Define Value *Lean Enterprise Institute calls this: Specifying Value* 1. Value is determined by the customer 2. Gather direct feedback and indirect feedback 3. Use the Net Promoter Score 4. Use Kano Analysis for Delighters and Dissatisfiers 5. Find out what annoys your customer, fix it and guarantee it	
1. Define the problem		
2. Grasp the Current Situation	Step 2: Map Your Current Process *Lean Enterprise Institute calls this: Map* 1. Go to the Gemba 2. Use Kaizen and Kaizen Meetings 3. Get started with a SIPOC 4. Create a Map of your Value Stream to Reveal Opportunities and Waste 5. Add Rework, VA/NVA Steps and Timings (Cycle time, Lead time, Takt time)	
3. Plan	Step 3: Reduce Wasteful Steps and Increase Flow *Lean Enterprise Institute calls this: Flow* 1. Eliminate any of the Eight Wastes 2. Use Pareto Analysis 3. Use Fishbone Analysis and the 5 Whys 4. Perform Line Balancing 5. Work towards One Piece Flow	

	Step 4: Use a Pull System and Build in Quality *Lean Enterprise Institute calls this: Pull* 1. Add Visual Management, FIFO and Kanban Triggers 2. Add Poka Yoke and Autonomation for Error Proofing 3. Level the Workload when Demand Fluctuates 4. Add 5S 5. Ensure Design for Ease of Use	
4. Do 5. Check 6. Act & Adjust 7. Lessons Learned	**Step 5: Create a New Standard Process and Improve Again** *Lean Enterprise Institute calls this: Perfection* 1. Create a Future State VSM and present to decision makers 2. Use an A3, LCA board and an Action Register 3. Use Agile for fast iterations and feedback 4. Create a Standard Operating Procedure and Checklist 5. Change incentives to reflect what you want	

The Five Minute Catch-up

One of the biggest challenges of a Lean transformation is getting everyone on the same page with the problem solving, job improving tools and methods, and creating a culture that supports it.

Epilogue

Having this book in everyone's hands is a good start, but if you want to ensure things move along quickly, you can use the "Five Minute Catch-up" to keep the method front of mind and increase your Lean momentum further.

As a Leader, it simply involves catching up with your team-mates for five minutes, once a week, and asking the questions below. The questions might seem simple, but they are designed with the "power of incentives" (5.5) in mind. Remember, what we measure, tends to improve. Asking these questions by catching up once a week is a friendly way to measure progress, and ensures the skills do not fade away. In practice, this might mean stopping by our team-mates' desk or workstation (the Gemba), or catching up at lunch or morning tea.

The questions are:

1. Where are you up to in the book?
2. What is your favourite part today?
3. Which part puzzles you?
4. What part(s) can you use currently to improve your own personal job?
5. How can I help you do this?

Other options might be to make the questions visible (on the wall or workstation) so everybody knows what to expect. Then team-mates, leaders, managers and even CEOs can stop by at any time and ask — everyone is on the same page.

If people aren't reading the book, or say they find it annoying or distasteful, don't worry! Disagreeing with something is how we come to understand it. Keep going routinely through the questions each week, and encourage team-mates to seek and discover answers for themselves. The problem solving culture will form, and you will find that the biggest critics often evolve into the greatest supporters.

The House of Lean

Keeping with the theme of seeing things at a glance, the House of Lean encompasses all of the Lean methodologies on a single page. If you keep this house diagram handy and review the tools in this book, you will notice all of them there in some capacity.

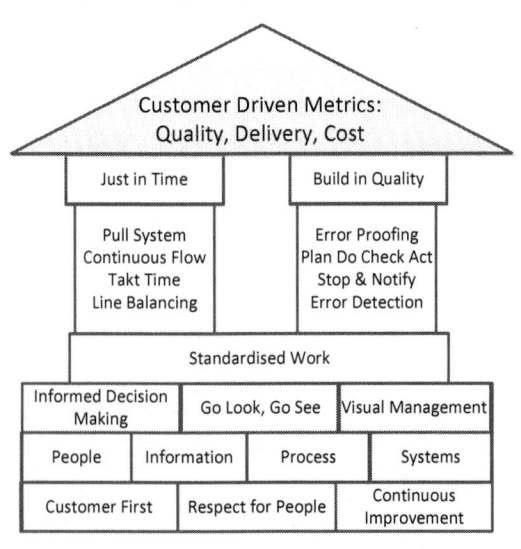

Customer Driven Metrics: Quality, Delivery, Cost			
Just in Time		Build in Quality	
Pull System, Continuous Flow, Takt Time, Line Balancing		Error Proofing, Plan Do Check Act, Stop & Notify, Error Detection	
Standardised Work			
Informed Decision Making	Go Look, Go See		Visual Management
People	Information	Process	Systems
Customer First	Respect for People		Continuous Improvement

A3 Template

Project Title

Date: / /

Sponsor	
Leader	
Facilitator	
Team Members	

Step 1 Due Date / /	Step 2 / /	Step 3 / /	Step 4 / /
Step 5 / /	Step 6 / /	Step 7 / /	Report Out / /

Step 1: Define The Problem

Include:
- Problem Statement: Make it measurable, based on the current standard, the expected results, and the gap between the two.
- Base it on improving the Customer Driven Metrics or reducing the eight wastes

Step 2: Grasp The Current Situation

Go to the Gemba, hold Kaizen meetings or events and include:
- SIPOCs,
- Value Stream Maps or,
- Swim Lane Flow Charts,
- Root Cause analysis with a Fishbone diagram and the Five Whys,
- Pareto Charts.

Step 3: Plan

Include:
- Root Causes,
- Brainstormed solutions,
- Action Register

#	Action Item	Assigned To:	Due Date
1			/ /
2			/ /
3			/ /
4			/ /

Step 4: Do

Have your team-members implement the plan in Step 3, and include:
- The details of the actual solution
- Document process or layout changes

Step 5: Check

Gather data from the changes and compare against targets in Step 3:

#	Measure	Baseline	Target	Actual	Rating
1					%
2					%
3					%
4					%

Step 6: Act (or Adjust)

If desired results are met:
- Document changes
- Update Standard Operating Procedures

If desired results are not met:
- Return to Step 3 – Plan

Step 7: Lessons Learned

Use the A3 to pass on lessons learned to others

Seven Step A3 Problem Solving Process

Step 1: Define the Problem
- Clearly define the problem you are working on, as a gap from the current performance to the desired performance,
- Base this gap on improving the Customer Driven Metrics (1.2) or reducing the eight wastes (3.1).
- If there is no standard process in place currently, either implement one before you proceed (based on the best performers) or articulate the current process using a Value Stream Map.

Step 2: Grasp the Current Situation
Find out the true situation by;
- Going to the Gemba (2.1),
- Creating a current state Value Stream Map (2.4) with important data (2.5) to reveal problems,
- Finding the biggest impacts with a Pareto Chart (3.2),
- Doing root cause analysis with a Fishbone diagram and the Five Whys (3.3).

Step 3: Plan
- Use a Pareto Chart on root causes to determine where to start (3.2).
- Brainstorm solutions to root causes with the team, based on chapters three and four (error proofing, making things visible, levelling and balancing the workload, having and supporting a standard process, using FIFO, working towards one piece flow, organising with 5S),
- Create an Action Register, with due dates, for team members to implement and follow up on solutions (5.2).

Step 4: Do
- Have team members implement the solutions with the Action Register (5.2).
- Make actions visible with a Kanban Board (5.3).
- Check in at the end of short iterations (5.3) and provide guidance where necessary.

Step 5: Check
- Measure the results from the baseline (current) against the target (expected), listing the actual result.

Step 6: Act and Adjust
- If your targets are met, then create a new Standard Operating Procedure outlining the new process (5.4).
- If your targets are not met, go back to Step 3 and adjust your solutions.

Step 7: Pass on Lessons Learned
- Can other departments, stores or companies learn a lesson from your solution?
- Use an A3 (5.2) to showcase the lessons you have learned.

Further Reading

The Toyota Way
By Jeffrey K. Liker
One of the best books out there on the Toyota Production System, also known as Lean, that breaks down not just the tools and how they are used, but the culture of its people and the principles of its management as well. Packed with plenty of real-life examples, this book is a true gem and will give you a deeper understanding when implementing Lean in your company.

The Toyota Way to Continuous Improvement
By Jeffrey K. Liker and James Franz
Building on the Lean management and culture building principles of The Toyota Way, nearly the last 300 pages of this book are pure real-life examples of Lean Senseis working to turn companies around, the methods that they used, the challenges they encountered and the lessons that they came away with.

The Gold Mine
By Michael Balle and Freddy Balle
A great story that subtly teaches Lean principles and methodologies, focussing on a company turn around and based on the methods in the original book to introduce the term Lean, "The Machine That Changed the World" by James Womack, Daniel Jones and Daniel Roos.

The Lean Manager
By Michael Balle and Freddy Balle
Another excellent story-based book on Lean, this one is based more on the management principles of "The Toyota Way" by Jeffrey Liker. It is a sequel to "The Gold Mine", but focusses on a manager and a CEO working together to implement Lean. It brings back some characters and introduces some new ones, and is an engaging read that imparts many excellent lessons.

EPILOGUE

Glossary of Lean Terms

5S
A method of organising a workplace to improve safety and efficiency. The 5S steps are: Sort, Straighten, Shine, Standardise, and Sustain.

5 Whys
A method of getting to the root cause of a problem, where we keep asking "why" until the real issue is revealed.

8 Wastes
Also "Muda" in Japanese, the eight wastes note the most common forms of waste in company processes that increase costs and inefficiencies. Our aim in Lean is to eliminate them all. They are: Defects, Over Production, Waiting, Non-use of Time and Talent, Transport, Inventory, Motion, and Excessive Processing. Two additional inefficiencies are Overburden (Muri) and Unevenness (Mura) in a process.

A3
An A3 is a single page that shows the details of a Lean implementation at a glance. It will include a clearly defined problem, then items from the "Plan, Do, Check, Act" cycle with analysis such as root cause diagrams, process maps, action registers and metrics for determining if the implementation is having the desired effect.

A/B Testing or Split Testing
Split testing is the method of testing different versions of the same product, message or process at the same time and gathering the results to determine which works better.

Agile
Agile is a method of implementing a project or change based on short, quick iterations in order to gather feedback as quickly as

possible. This allows us to determine if our project is on the right track so we can either continue or adjust.

Andon
A Japanese term for "light" and a part of Visual Management, an Andon is where the status of a process or operation is shown at a glance, using a light, such as with green (for go) or red (for stop) signals.

Autonomation (Jidoka)
Where machines and/or team-mates have the ability to detect when something is wrong and immediately stop work, so the root cause can be found quickly and solved.

Batch Processing
The enemy of Lean and smooth flowing processes, this is a mass production approach where product is created regardless of whether it is required, and often results in overproduction and waste.

Capabilities, the Four
As defined by Steven Spear in "The High Velocity Edge", the Four Capabilities were found to be in high performing leaders and are as follows: designing their work to reveal problems & opportunities, swarming those problems to solve them and build new knowledge, sharing that knowledge throughout the organisation, and developing the first three skills in everyone else.

Chunking
Chunking is the process of taking a large problem or project and breaking it into chunks to make it easier to solve or implement.

Customer
A "customer" in Lean terms is defined as any process downstream from the current one. The end customer, of course, is the one who ultimately buys a product or service.

Cycle time
The total time it takes to complete a process step within our value stream.

FIFO Lane
First-In-First-Out lane, where items that come in first ultimately go out first.

Fishbone Diagram
Also known as an Ishikawa diagram, this is a method of getting to the root cause of a problem where you note the effect or problem at the "head" of the fish, then the causes you can think of under the "bones" of People, Information, Process or Systems. Similar causes are grouped and whichever group has the most causes is typically looked at first.

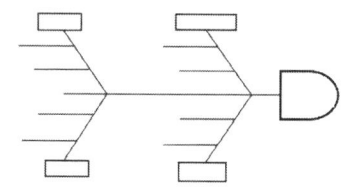

Flow
The Flow of a process is how well it moves continuously from upstream to downstream processes. Improving Flow involves reducing wasteful steps or interruptions and improving efficiency from the time a customer places an order to the time a product or service is completed and delivered.

Gemba
The Gemba is the Japanese term for "Actual Place" and is often used as a single word to describe the front lines where the work is done. In English it can also be spelled Genba. "Walking the Gemba" is a large part of Lean which means we must go to where the work is done to get the real answers and not rely on reports or second hand information.

Jidoka
See *Autonomation*

Just in Time
Just in Time is a system of production that makes and delivers only what is needed, when it is needed. It combines five Lean elements for success: Takt time or customer demand, Continuous Flow, a Pull System, Line Balancing, and removing Waste.

Kaizen and Kaizen Events
Kaizen is the Japanese term for "Improvement" and is most often referred to in English as continuous improvement. A Kaizen meeting or event, therefore, is an improvement meeting where we go through the "Plan, Do, Check, Act" process or the five steps outlined in this book.

Kanban
Literally "sign" or "sign-board" in Japanese, Kanban in its many forms is most used as a trigger for upstream suppliers to produce more product.

Kanban Board
Used in Agile, a Kanban Board is a visual way to manage work and consists of cards with small pieces of work on them assigned to a team-member and moved along columns such as "To Do", In Progress", and "Done". Columns can also be named depending on your own work phases or departments.

To do:	In progress:	Done:
Item 1	Item 3	
Item 4	Item 5	Item 2

Kano Analysis

Kano analysis divides customer feedback (the Voice of the Customer) into Dissatisfiers, Satisfiers and Delighters where the aim is to increase Delighters and remove Dissatisfiers.

Kata

Brought to the world's attention in "Toyota Kata" by Mike Rother, Kata involves three main steps:
1. Grasping the current situation,
2. Defining the desired situation, then;
3. Moving toward that goal in iterations so as to uncover feedback or obstacles.

LCA Board

A Layered Check Act board is a method of visual management. Usually a board will be at least one to two meters in diameter, and it shows the metrics of a current process measured against the proposed targets. If the metrics are not meeting these targets, then countermeasures are added (often after a Lean initiative) to assist in bringing them into line.

Lead Time

The total time it takes to create your product or service from the moment the customer orders to the time it is delivered, including both Value-Add and Non-Value-Add time.

Line Balancing

Line Balancing is based on the premise that a process is only as fast as its slowest step. Based on this, in many cases we can combine faster processes together, provided they are still faster than Takt time or customer demand. This means we can also split longer steps up to ensure they are under Takt time.

Net Promoter Score

The Net Promoter Score is from the book "The Ultimate Question 2.0", where we ask our customer "On a scale of 1 to 10, how likely are you to recommend our product / service to a friend?" The results are often used in conjunction with Kano Analysis.

Overburden (Muri)
Overburden or Muri is where team-mates or equipment are required to work harder, faster or more than is necessary, often because of wasteful steps or processes.

Pareto Chart
A Pareto chart is based on the idea that 80% of results come from approximately 20% of the effort. It shows item measurements in a bar chart, and the cumulative percentage in a line graph overlaying the chart. In this way, we can see which items will have the greatest impact when fixed, and focus on these first.

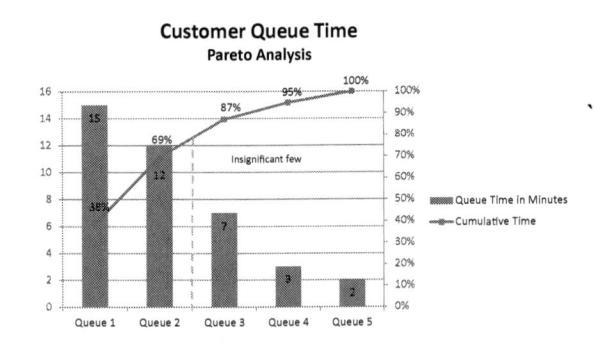

Poka Yoke
"Error-Proofing" in Japanese, this means putting steps in place to make it impossible to make a mistake. A USB cable and port, or an electric plug is a good example of this.

Problem Charter
Problem charters are often created at the beginning of a larger project. They often include: The stated problem, the current

situation, the impact it has, the stakeholders or problem owners and any team members assigned to the problem.

Pull

A Pull System is one where downstream departments signal their needs to upstream activities (often using a Kanban), allowing them to pull work in accordance with demand.

Push

The opposite of Pull, where upstream departments create product regardless of demand, and push it through to their downstream customers. This can result in waste such as over-production, over-burden and over-processing.

Silo

A silo in a company is when a management system, process or department is cut off from the rest of the business or unable to communicate with other sources of company information. This can result in misinformation, miscommunication, slower processes and lower morale.

SIPOC

A SIPOC chart shows the Suppliers, process Inputs, Process steps, process Outputs, and Customers. We can also add Customer Requirements, and Measures of a process as well. It gives a "high level" view of the process steps, and is a good foundation for other tools on larger projects, especially when we need to know the stakeholders involved.

SMED / Quick Changeover Techniques

Single Minute Exchange of Dies (SMED) is a process of changing over equipment (or people, stations, or anything else you might think of) from one to another in as little time as possible. It is based on Internal changeover operations that can only be done when the process is stopped, and External operations that can be done while the process is still going. The aim then becomes to convert all Internal changeover operations to

External changeover operations to simplify and speed up the changeover process.

SOP
A Standard Operating Procedure (SOP) is a standard, repeatable way of carrying out a process. Often in writing and better still in the form of a checklist, using a SOP ensures staff operate the same way. It makes it easier to train, easier to quality check and helps reduce single points of failure if staff are sick or on holidays.

Spaghetti Diagram
A Spaghetti Diagram is a diagram of a production floor with lines following the product as it travels through the steps or workstations. Often initially a diagram will look like cooked spaghetti as the product goes back and forth and around a workspace. Simplifying this movement can significantly reduce waste.

Supermarket
A Supermarket in Lean terms is a predetermined standard inventory kept to supply a downstream process. Keeping no more than is needed, when a supermarket is empty a Kanban is often sent to the supplier to replenish the standard inventory.

Supplier
Any workstation, department, person or company that is upstream from the current process.

Swim Lane Chart
A flow chart of process steps where departments or stations are noted vertically, and the steps are noted horizontally. In this way, we can clearly see movement between departments and potential wastes.

Takt Time
The product demand time as determined by the Customer. For example if a Customer buys 80 items in an 8 hour work day, our Takt Time is 10 items an hour.

TPM
Total Productive Maintenance (TPM) is a set of techniques to improve usability and longevity of machines. It involves cleaning and repairing, performing error proofing, developing a maintenance database and a standard process for continuing maintenance in the future.

Unevenness (Mura)
Unevenness or "Mura" in an operation is when a process has excessive wait time followed by excessively busy periods. In other words, team-mates are forced to "hurry and then wait". Not only does Unevenness in a process reduce morale, it is often a wasteful use of team-mates' time and resources. Unevenness can be reduced by using Line Balancing, working towards One Piece Flow, and reducing Rework in a process.

Value
Value is always defined by the Customer, and in its purest form it is something within a process that a Customer is willing to pay for. For example making a product's process simpler may not directly add value to a customer, however the cost reduction, speed of delivery, and increase in quality or savings to a customer will.

Value Stream
A Value Stream is the process of creating our product or service — it is the "stream" of process steps that create our product to bring value to the customer.

Value Stream Map
Also known as a VSM, this is the standard method of mapping out a process, often including the Suppliers and Customer,

Systems, Process Steps, Process Timings, Rework and any other useful information.

A "Future State VSM" is created when you have analysed a current process and want to show the new process with added value and without the waste.

VOC

The Voice of the Customer (VOC) refers to data captured around customer metrics or feedback.

Work in Process

Also known as Standard Inventory, it is the minimum number of items or parts (including parts in machines or queues) needed to keep a workstation or department flowing smoothly. A Supermarket is a good example of this.

Made in the USA
Lexington, KY
22 July 2019